I will run
in the way of thy commandments
when thou enlargest
my understanding!
Psalm 119:32

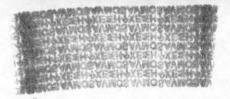

Other books by Eugene H. Peterson

Run with the Horses

Horses

Eugene H. Peterson

The Quest for Life at Its Best

InterVarsity Press
Downers Grove
Illinois 60515

InterVarsity Press is the book-publishing division of Inter-Varsity Christian Fellowship, a student movement active on campus at hundreds of universities, colleges and schools of nursing. For information about local and regional activities, write IVCF, 233 Langdon St., Madison, WI 53703.

Distributed in Canada through InterVarsity Press, 860 Denison St., Unit 3, Markham, Ontario L3R 4H1, Canada.

All biblical quotations, unless otherwise noted, are from the Revised Standard Version of the Bible copyrighted 1946, 1952, © 1971, 1973, and used by permission.

The poem "What I expected was," found on p. 32, is from Collected Poems 1928-1953 *by Stephen Spender, copyright 1934 and renewed 1962 by Stephen Spender. Reprinted by permission from Random House, Inc., and Faber and Faber, Ltd.*

Cover photograph: Robert McKendrick

ISBN 0-87784-905-6

Printed in the United States of America

Library of Congress Cataloging in Publication Data

Peterson, Eugene H., 1932-
    Run with the horses.

    Includes bibliographical references.
    1. Jeremiah.   2. Bible. O.T. Jeremiah–
Meditations.   I. Title.
BS580.J4P47 1983   242'.5   83-13005
ISBN 0-87784-905-6

17	16	15	14	13	12	11	10	9	8	7	6	5	4	3	2	1
96	95	94	93	92	91	90	89	88	87	86	85	84	83			

For Eric
also the son of a priest

1 How Will You Compete with Horses?

If you have raced with men on foot, and they have wearied you,
how will you compete with horses?
And if in a safe land you fall down,
how will you do in the jungle of the Jordan?

Jeremiah 12:5

My grievance with contemporary society is with its decrepitude. There are few towering pleasures to allure me, almost no beauty to bewitch me, nothing erotic to arouse me, no intellectual circles or positions to challenge or provoke me, no burgeoning philosophies or theologies and no new art to catch my attention or engage my mind, no arousing political, social, or religious movements to stimulate or excite me. There are no free men to lead me. No saints to inspire me. No sinners sinful enough to either impress me or share my plight. No one human enough to validate the "going" lifestyle. It is hard to linger in that dull world without being dulled.

I stake the future on the few humble and hearty lovers who seek God passionately in the marvelous, messy world of redeemed and related realities that lie in front of our noses.

William McNamara[1]

The puzzle is why so many people live so badly. Not so wickedly, but so inanely. Not so cruelly, but so stupidly. There is little to admire and less to imitate in the people who are prominent in our culture. We have celebrities but not saints. Famous entertainers amuse a nation of bored insomniacs. Infamous criminals act out the aggressions of timid conformists. Petulant and spoiled athletes play games vicariously for lazy and apathetic spectators. People, aimless and bored, amuse themselves with trivia and trash. Neither the adventure of goodness nor the pursuit of righteousness gets headlines.

Modern man is "a bleak business," says Tom Howard. "To our chagrin we discover that the declaration of autonomy has issued not in a race of free, masterly men, but rather in a race that can be described by its poets and dramatists only as bored, vexed, frantic, embittered, and sniffling."[2]

This condition has produced an odd phenomenon: individuals who live trivial lives and then engage in evil acts in order to establish significance for themselves. Assassins and hijackers attempt the gigantic leap from obscurity to fame by killing a prominent person or endangering the lives of an airplane full of passengers. Often they are successful. The mass media report their words and display their actions. Writers vie with one another in analyzing their motives and providing psychological profiles on them. No other culture has been as eager to reward either nonsense or wickedness.

If, on the other hand, we look around for what it means to be a mature, whole, blessed person, we don't find much. These people are around, maybe as many of them as ever, but they aren't easy to pick out. No journalist interviews them. No talk show features them. They are not admired. They are not looked up to. They do not set trends. There is no cash value in them. No Oscars are given for integrity. At year's end no one compiles a list of the ten best-lived lives.

A Thirst for Wholeness

All the same, we continue to have an unquenchable thirst for wholeness, a hunger for righteousness. When we get thoroughly disgusted with the shams and cretins that are served up to us daily as celebrities, some of us turn to Scripture to satisfy our need for someone to look up to. What does it mean to be a real man, a real woman? What shape does mature, authentic humanity take in everyday life?

When we do turn to Scripture for help in this matter we are apt to be surprised. One of the first things that strikes us about the men and women in Scripture is that they were disappointingly nonheroic. We do not find splendid moral examples. We do not find impeccably virtuous models. That always comes as a shock to newcomers to Scripture: Abraham lied; Jacob cheated; Moses murdered and complained; David committed adultery; Peter blasphemed.

We read on and begin to suspect intention: a consistent strategy to demonstrate that the great, significant figures in the life of faith were fashioned from the same clay as the rest of us. We find that Scripture is sparing in the information that it gives on people while it is lavish in what it tells us about God. It refuses to feed our lust for hero worship. It will not pander to our adolescent desire to join a fan club. The reason is, I think, clear enough. Fan clubs encourage secondhand living. Through pictures and memorabilia, autographs and tourist visits, we associate with someone whose life is (we think) more exciting and glamorous than our own. We find diversion from our own humdrum existence by riding on the coattails of someone exotic.

We do it because we are convinced that we are plain and ordinary. The town or city that we live in, the neighborhood we grew up in, the friends we are stuck with, the families or marriages that we have—all seem undramatic. We see no way to be significant in such settings, with such associations, so we surround ourselves with evidence of someone who is. We stock our fantasies with images of a person who is living more adventurously than we are. And we have enterprising people around who provide us (for a fee, of course) with the material to fuel the fires of this vicarious living. There is something sad and pitiful about the whole business. But it flourishes nonetheless.

Scripture, however, doesn't play that game. Something very different takes place in the life of faith: each person discovers all the elements of a unique and original adventure. We are prevented from following in another's footsteps and are called to an incomparable association with Christ. The Bible makes it clear that every time that there is a story of faith, it is completely original. God's creative genius is endless. He never, fatigued and unable to maintain the rigors of creativity, resorts to mass-producing copies. Each life is a fresh canvas on which he uses lines and colors, shades and lights, textures and proportions that he has never used before.

We see *what* is possible: anyone and everyone is able to live a zestful life that spills out of the stereotyped containers that a sin-inhibited society provides. Such lives fuse spontaneity and purpose and green the desiccated landscape with meaning. And we see *how* it is possible: by plunging into a life of faith, participating in what God initiates in each life, exploring what God is doing in each event. The persons we meet on the pages of Scripture are remarkable for the intensity with which they live Godwards, the thoroughness in which all the details of their lives are included in God's

word to them, in God's action in them. It is these persons, who are conscious of participating in what God is saying and doing, who are most human, most alive. These persons are evidence that none of us is required to live "at this
poor dying rate" for another day, another hour.

An Image of Man

This two-edged quality of Scripture—the capacity to inten-
sify a passion for excellence combined with an indifference
to human achievement as such—strikes me with particular
force in the book of Jeremiah.

Cleanth Brooks wrote, "One looks for an image of man,
attempting in a world increasingly dehumanized to realize
himself as a man—to act like a responsible moral being, not
to drift like a mere thing."[3] Jeremiah, for me, is such an
"image of man," a life of excellence, what the Greeks called
aretē. In Jeremiah it is clear that the excellence comes from a
life of faith, from being more interested in God than in
self, and has almost nothing to do with comfort or esteem
or achievement. Here is a person who lived life to the hilt,
but there is not a hint of human pride or worldly success
or personal achievement in the story. Jeremiah arouses my
passion for a full life. At the same time he firmly shuts the
door against attempts to achieve it through self-promotion,
self-gratification or self-improvement.

It is enormously difficult to portray goodness in an attractive way; it is much easier to make a scoundrel interest-
ing. All of us have so much more experience in sin than in
goodness that a writer has far more imaginative material to
work with in presenting a bad character than a good person. In novels and poems and plays most of the memorable
figures are either villains or victims. Good people, virtuous
lives, mostly seem a bit dull. Jeremiah is a stunning exception. For most of my adult life he has attracted me. The
complexity and intensity of his person caught and kept my

attention. The captivating quality in the man is his goodness, his virtue, his excellence. He lived at his best. His was
not a hot-house piety, for he lived through crushing storms
of hostility and furies of bitter doubt. There is not a trace
of smugness or complacency or naiveté in Jeremiah—every
muscle in his body was stretched to the limits by fatigue,
every thought in his mind subjected to rejection, every feeling in his heart put through fires of ridicule. Goodness in
Jeremiah was not "being nice." It was something more like
prowess.

Jeremiah has thus served personal needs. But he has also
been of pastoral importance, and the personal and pastoral
interests converge. As a pastor I encourage others to live at
their best and provide guidance in doing it. But how do I do
this without inadvertently inciting pride and arrogance?
How do I stimulate an appetite for excellence without feeding at the same time a selfish determination to elbow anyone aside who gets in the way? Insistent encouragement is
given by many voices today for living a better life. I welcome
the encouragement. But the counsel that accompanies the
encouragement has introduced no end of mischief into our
society, and I am in strenuous opposition to it. The counsel
is that we can arrive at our full humanness by gratifying
our desires. It has been a recipe for misery for millions.[4]
The biblical counsel in these matters is clear: "not my will
but thine be done." But how do I guide people to deny self
without having that misunderstood as encouraging them to
be doormats on which people wipe their feet? The difficult
pastoral art is to encourage people to grow in excellence
and to live selflessly, at one and the same time to lose the self
and find the self. It is paradoxical, but it is not impossible.
And Jeremiah is preeminent among those who have done
it—a fully developed self (and therefore extraordinarily
attractive) and a thoroughly selfless person (and therefore
maturely wise). In conversations, in lectures, on retreats, in

sermons, Jeremiah has, for twenty-five years now, been example and mentor for me.

A Quest for the Best
We live in a society that tries to diminish us to the level of the antheap so that we scurry mindlessly, getting and consuming. It is essential to take counteraction. Jeremiah is counteraction: a well-developed human being, mature and robust, living by faith. My procedure here is to select the biographical parts of the book of Jeremiah and reflect on them personally and pastorally in the context of present, everyday life. More is known of the life of Jeremiah than of any other prophet, and his life is far more significant than his teaching.[5] It is noteworthy, I think, that when people were trying to account for Jesus, Jeremiah was one of the names put forward (Mt 16:14). By enlisting the devout imagination in meditatively perusing these pages of Scripture, I hope to stir up a dissatisfaction with anything less than our best. I want to provide fresh documentation that the only way that any one of us can live at our best is in a life of radical faith in God. Every one of us needs to be stretched to live at our best, awakened out of dull moral habits, shaken out of petty and trivial busy-work. Jeremiah does that for me. And not only for me. Millions upon millions of Christians and Jews have been goaded and guided toward excellence as they have attended to God's word spoken to and by Jeremiah.

I have arranged the passages that I have chosen for reflection in roughly chronological order. The book of Jeremiah is not itself arranged chronologically, and there is far more in it than biography. That means that readers not infrequently puzzle over transitions and wrestle to find the appropriate settings for the sayings. I have not attempted to sort out these puzzles or explain the difficulties. Nor have I described the complex international historical background of the times, a knowledge of which is an immense help in reading Jeremiah. That would be to write another kind of book and a much longer one. For readers who want to extend their understanding of Jeremiah and be guided through the text in detail, I recommend three books: R. K. Harrison, *Jeremiah and Lamentations* (InterVarsity Press) for a good, readable introduction into the world and text of Jeremiah; John A. Thompson, *The Book of Jeremiah* (Eerdmans) for a more advanced, detailed treatment; and John Bright, *Jeremiah* (Doubleday) for the most complete study of the prophet and the prophecy.

Competing with Horses

Vitezslav Gardavsky, the Czech philosopher and martyr who died in 1978, took Jeremiah as his "image of man" in his campaign against a society that carefully planned every detail of material existence but eliminated mystery and miracle, and squeezed all freedom from life. The terrible threat against life, he said in his book *God Is Not Yet Dead,* is not death, nor pain, nor any variation on the disasters that we so obsessively try to protect ourselves against with our social systems and personal stratagems. The terrible threat is "that we might die earlier than we really do die, before death has become a natural necessity. The real horror lies in just such a *premature* death, a death after which we go on living for many years."[6]

There is a memorable passage concerning Jeremiah's life when, worn down by the opposition and absorbed in self-pity, he was about to capitulate to just such a premature death. He was ready to abandon his unique calling in God and settle for being a Jerusalem statistic. At that critical moment he heard the reprimand: "If you have raced with men on foot, and they have wearied you, how will you compete with horses? And if in a safe land you fall down, how will you do in the jungle of the Jordan?" (Jer 12:5). Biochemist Erwin Chargaff updates the questions: "What do you want to achieve? Greater riches? Cheaper chicken? A happier life, a longer life? Is it power over your neighbors that you are after? Are you only running away from your death? Or are you seeking greater wisdom, deeper piety?"[7]

Life is difficult, Jeremiah. Are you going to quit at the first wave of opposition? Are you going to retreat when you find that there is more to life than finding three meals a day and a dry place to sleep at night? Are you going to run home the minute you find that the mass of men and women are more interested in keeping their feet warm than in living at risk to the glory of God? Are you going to live cautiously or courageously? I called you to live at your best, to pursue righteousness, to sustain a drive toward excellence. It is easier, I know, to be neurotic. It is easier to be parasitic. It is easier to relax in the embracing arms of The Average. Easier, but not better. Easier, but not more significant. Easier, but not more fulfilling. I called you to a life of purpose far beyond what you think yourself capable of living and promised you adequate strength to fulfill your destiny. Now at the first sign of difficulty you are ready to quit. If you are fatigued by this run-of-the-mill crowd of apathetic mediocrities, what will you do when the real race starts, the race with the swift and determined horses of excellence? What is it you really want, Jeremiah, do you want to shuffle along with this crowd, or run with the horses?

It is understandable that there are retreats from excellence, veerings away from risk, withdrawals from faith. It is easier to define oneself minimally ("a featherless biped") and live securely within that definition than to be defined maximally ("little less than God") and live adventurously in that reality. It is unlikely, I think, that Jeremiah was spontaneous or quick in his reply to God's question. The ecstatic ideals for a new life had been splattered with the world's cynicism. The euphoric impetus of youthful enthusiasm no longer carried him. He weighed the options. He counted the cost. He tossed and turned in hesitation. The response when it came was not verbal but biographical. His life became his answer, "I'll run with the horses."

2 Jeremiah

The words of Jeremiah, the son of Hilkiah, of the priests who were in Anathoth in the land of Benjamin, to whom the word of the LORD came...

Jeremiah 1:1-2

What's in a name? The history of the human race is in names. Our objective friends do not understand that, since they move in a world of objects which can be counted and numbered. They reduce the great names of the past to dust and ashes. This they call scientific history. But the whole meaning of history is in the proof that there have lived people before the present time whom it is important to meet.

Eugen Rosenstock-Huessy[1]

The first thing that I can remember wanting to be when I grew up was an Indian fighter. Only a couple of generations before I was born the area in which I grew up was Indian country. I could walk from my house into the foothills of the Rocky Mountains in about twenty minutes. On most Saturdays through my boyhood years I carried a lunch with me and roamed for the day in those hills, exploring forests and streams, imagining myself matching wits with treacherous Indians.

If anyone would have pressed me to account for what I was doing on those rambles, I'm not sure I could have done it, but the feelings are still sharp and vivid in my memory: a feeling of adventure in the wilderness in contrast to the protected and prosaic life in the town; a feeling of goodness in contest with evil, for in those days the only Indian stories I had heard featured them scalping innocent travelers.

All the great stories of the world elaborate one of two themes: that all life is an exploration like that of the *Odyssey* or that all life is a battle like that of the *Iliad*. The stories of Odysseus and Achilles are archetypal. Everyone's childhood serves up the raw material that is shaped by grace into the life of mature faith.

I had most of my facts wrong on those wonderful Saturdays. The wilderness that I thought I was exploring was owned by the Great Northern Railroad and was already plotted for destruction by executives in a New York City skyscraper; the Indians that I supposed were darkly murderous were, I learned later, noble and generous, themselves victims of rapacious early settlers. My facts were wrong; all the same there were two things essentially right about what I experienced. One, there was far more to existence than had been presented to me in home and school, in the streets and alleys of my town, and it was important to find out what it was, to reach out and explore. Two, life was a contest of good against evil and the battle was for the highest stakes—the winning of good over evil, of blessing over malignity. Life is a continuous exploration of ever more reality. Life is a constant battle against everyone and anything that corrupts or diminishes its reality.

After a few years of wandering those hills and never finding any Indians, I realized that there was not much of a market any longer for Indian fighters. I was forced to abandon that fantasy, and I did it readily enough when the time came, for I have always found that realities are better in the long run than fantasies. At the same time I found myself under pressure to abandon the accompanying convictions that life is an adventure and that life is a contest. I was not, and am not, willing to do that.

Some people as they grow up become less. As children they have glorious ideas of who they are and of what life has for them. Thirty years later we find that they have settled for something grubby and inane. What accounts for the exchange of childhood aspiration to the adult anemia?

Other people as they grow up become more. Life is not an inevitable decline into dullness; for some it is an ascent into excellence. It was for Jeremiah. Jeremiah lived about sixty years. Across that life span there is no sign of decay or shriveling. Always he was pushing out the borders of reality, exploring new territory. And always he was vigorous in battle, challenging and contesting the shoddy, the false, the vile.

How did he do it? How do I do it? How do I shed the fantasies of boyhood and simultaneously increase my hold on the realities of life? How do I leave the childish yet keep the deeply accurate perceptions of the child—that life is an adventure, that life is a contest?

What's in a Name?

The book of Jeremiah begins with a personal name, *Jeremiah*. Seven more personal names follow: Hilkiah, Benjamin, Josiah, Amon, Judah, Jehoiakim, Zedekiah. The personal name is the most important part of speech in our language. The cluster of personal names that opens the book of Jeremiah strikes exactly the right note for what is most characteristic of Jeremiah: the personal in contrast to the stereotyped role, the individual in contrast to the blurred crowd, the unique spirit in contrast to generalized cultural moods. The book in which we find this most memorable record of what it means to be human in the fullest, most developed sense, begins with personal names.

Naming focuses the essential. The act of naming, an act that occurs early in everyone's life, has enormous significance. We are named. From that sextant a life course is plotted on the oceans of reality in pursuit of righteousness. Eugen Rosenstock-Huessy has mined the meaning of naming: "The name is the state of speech in which we do not speak of people or things or values, but in which we speak *to* people, things, and values. . . . The name is the right address of a person under which he or she will respond. The original meaning of language was this very fact that it could be used to make people respond."[2]

At our birth we are named, not numbered. The name is that part of speech by which we are recognized as a person. We are not classified as a species of animal. We are not labeled as a compound of chemicals. We are not assessed for our economic potential and given a cash value. We are named. What we are named is not as significant as *that* we are named.

Jeremiah's impressive stature as a human being—Ewald calls him the "most human prophet"[3]—and the developing vitality of that humanness for sixty years have their source in his naming, along with the centered seriousness with which he took his name and the names of others. "To be called by his true name is part of any listener's process of becoming his true self. We have to receive a name by others; this is part of the process of being fully born."[4] Jeremiah was named and immersed in names. He was never reduced to a role or absorbed into a sociological trend or catapulted into a historical crisis. His identity and significance developed from the event of naming and his response to naming. The world of Jeremiah does not open with a description of the scenery or a sketch of the culture but with eight personal names.

Any time that we move from personal names to abstract labels or graphs or statistics, we are less in touch with reality and diminished in our capacity to deal with what is best and at the center of life. Yet we are encouraged on every side to do just that. In many areas of life the accurate transmission of our social-security number is more important than the integrity with which we live. In many sectors of the economy the title that we hold is more important than our ability to do certain work. In many situations the public image that people have of us is more important than the personal relations that we develop with them. Every time that we go along with this movement from the personal to the impersonal, from the immediate to the remote, from the concrete to the abstract, we are diminished, we are less. Resistance is required if we will retain our humanity.

"It is a spiritual disaster," warned Thomas Merton, "for a man to rest content with his exterior identity, with his passport picture of himself. Is his life merely in his fingerprints?"[5] But passport pictures, more likely than not, are preferred, even required, in most of our dealings in the world.

In preparing for travel to another continent I applied for a passport. I presented my birth certificate with the application. The clerk in the post office to whom I presented the document was a man I had known by name for nineteen years. He refused the application: I had not presented the original birth certificate but a photocopy. I brought in the original; that also was rejected; it had to be embossed. I wrote to the state in which I was born and purchased an embossed copy. All this time I was dealing with a person who knew my name and had observed my life in the community for nineteen years. That personal, firsthand knowledge was rejected in favor of an impersonal document.

I think that I can reconstruct the steps that result in such procedures. There is danger of foreign espionage. Our government has a responsibility for keeping our nation safe. It would be unreliable to depend on the personal loyalty and knowledge of a post-office worker to determine identities. Insisting on an embossed birth certificate is a way of guarding against forgeries.

In my situation the procedure was not so much frustrating as amusing. But the incident itself, a minor inconvenience, is symptomatic of a major danger to our humanity: if I am frequently and authoritatively treated impersonally, I begin to think of myself the same way. I consider myself in terms of how I fit into the statistical norms; I evaluate myself in terms of my usefulness; I assess my worth in response to how much others want me or don't want me. In the process of going along with such procedures I find myself defined by a label, squeezed into a role, functioning at the level of my social-security number. It requires assertive, lifelong effort to keep our names in front. Our names are far more important than trends in the economy, far more important than crises in the cities, far more important than breakthroughs in space travel. For a name addresses the uniquely human creature. A name recognizes that I am this person and not another.

No one can assess my significance by looking at the work that I do. No one can determine my worth by deciding the

salary they will pay me. No one can know what is going on in
my mind by examining my school transcripts. No one can
know me by measuring me or weighing me or analyzing
me. Call my name.

A Way of Hoping

Names not only address what we are, the irreplaceably
human, they also anticipate what we become. Names call us
to become who we will be. A lifetime of growth and development is announced by a name. Names *mean* something.
A personal name designates what is irreducibly personal;
it also calls us to become what we are not yet.

The meaning of a name is not discovered through schol-
arly etymology or through meditative introspection. It is
not validated by bureaucratic approval. And it certainly is
not worked up through the vanity of public relations. The
meaning of a name is not in the dictionary, not in the unconscious, not in the size of the lettering. It is in *relationship*
—with God. It was the Jeremiah "to whom the word of the
LORD came" who realized his authentic and eternal being.

Naming is a way of hoping. We name a child after someone or some quality that we hope he or she will become—a
saint, a hero, an admired ancestor. Some parents name
their children trivially after movie stars and millionaires.
Harmless? Cute? But we do have a way of taking on the
identities that are prescribed for us. Millions live out
the superficial sham of the entertainer and the greedy ex-
ploitiveness of the millionaire because, in part, significant
people in their lives cast them in a role or fantasized an
illusion and failed to hope a human future for them.

When I take an infant into my arms at the baptismal font
and ask the parents, "What is the Christian name of this
child?" I am not only asking, "Who is this child I am holding?" but also, "What do you want this child to become?
What are your visions for this life?" George Herbert knew

the evocative power of naming when he instructed his fellow pastors in sixteenth-century England that at baptism they "admit no vain or idle names."[6]

Yoknapatawpha County, Mississippi, is the region created by novelist William Faulkner to show the spiritual and moral condition of life in our times. An examination of the men and women who live there is a powerful incentive to the imagination to realize both the comic and tragic aspects of what is going on among us as we make it (or don't make it) through life. One of the children is named Montgomery Ward. Montgomery Ward Snopes.[7] It is the perfect name for the child being trained to be a successful consumer. If you want your child to grow up getting and spending, using available leisure in the shopping malls, proving virility by getting things, that is the right name: Montgomery Ward Snopes, patron saint of the person for whom the ritual of shopping is the new worship, the department store the new cathedral, and the advertising page the infallible Scripture.

One of the supreme tasks of the faith community is to announce to us early and clearly the kind of life into which we can grow, to help us set our sights on what it means to be a human being complete. Not one of us, at this moment, is complete. In another hour, another day, we will have changed. We are in process of becoming either less or more. There are a million chemical and electrical interchanges going on in each of us this very moment. There are intricate moral decisions and spiritual transactions taking place. What are we becoming? Less or more?

John, writing to an early community of Christians, said, "Beloved, we are God's children now; it does not yet appear what we shall be, but we know that when he appears we shall be like him, for we shall see him as he is" (1 Jn 3:2). We *are* children; we *will be* adults. We can see what we are now; we are children of God. We don't yet see the results of what we are becoming, but we know the goal, to be like Christ, or,

in Paul's words, to arrive at "mature manhood, to the measure of the stature of the fulness of Christ" (Eph 4:13). We
do not deteriorate. We do not disintegrate. We *become*.

William Stafford was once asked in an interview, "When
did you decide to be a poet?" He responded that the question was put wrongly: everyone is born a poet—a person
discovering the way words sound and work, caring and delighting in words. I just kept on doing, he said, what everyone starts out doing. "The real question is why did the other
people stop?"[8]

Jeremiah kept on doing what everybody starts out doing,
being human. And he didn't stop. For sixty years and more
he continued to live into the meaning of his name. The
exact meaning of *Jeremiah* is not certain: it may mean "the
LORD exalts"; it may mean "the LORD hurls." What is certain is that "the LORD," the personal name of God, is in his
name.

On the day that their son was born, Hilkiah and his wife
named him in anticipation of the way that God would act in
his life. In hope they saw the years unfolding and their son
as one in whom the Lord would be lifted up: *Jeremiah*—the
Lord is exalted. Or, in hope they saw into the future and
anticipated their son as a person whom God would hurl
into the community as a javelin-representative of God,
penetrating the defenses of selfishness with divine judgment and mercy: *Jeremiah*—the Lord hurls. Either way, it is
clear that God is in the name. Jeremiah's life was compounded with God's action. Jeremiah's parents saw their
child as a region of being in which the human and divine
would integrate. The life of God in some way or other
(exalting? hurling?) would find expression in this child of
theirs. Naming is not a whim; it is a lever of hope against the
future. And the "hope is not a dream but a way of making
dreams become reality" (Cardinal L. J. Suenens).

No child is just a child. Each is a creature in whom God

intends to do something glorious and great. No one is only a product of the genes contributed by parents. Who we are and will be is compounded with who God is and what he does. God's love and providence and salvation are comprised in the reality of our existence along with our metabolism and blood type and fingerprints.

Most names throughout Israel's history were compounded with the name of God. The names anticipated what each would be when he, when she, grew up. *Josiah,* God heals; *Jehoiakim,* the Lord raises up; *Zedekiah,* the Lord is righteous; *Jeremiah,* the Lord exalts, or the Lord hurls. Some of these people lived out the meaning of their names. Jeremiah and Josiah did. Others, like Jehoiakim and Zedekiah, were an embarrassment to their names, parodying with their lives the great promise of their names. Zedekiah had a glorious name; he betrayed it. Jehoiakim had a superb name; he abandoned it.

There were at least three categories into which Jeremiah could have quietly slipped, taking his place among the religious professionals of his day: prophet, priest or wise man. These were the accepted roles for persons who had concern for the things of God and the ways of humanity. Jeremiah's refusal to accept any of the available roles and his eccentric insistence on living out the identity of his name put him in conspicuous contrast to the eroded smoothness of those who were shaped by the expectations of popular opinion and who gathered content for their messages not by asking "What is there to eat?" but "What will Jones swallow?" His angular integrity exposed the shallow complacencies in which they lived. They were provoked and then enraged: "Come, let us make plots against Jeremiah, for the law shall not perish from the priest, nor counsel from the wise, nor the word from the prophet. Come, let us smite him with the tongue, and let us not heed any of his words" (Jer 18:18). Priest and wise man and prophet alike felt that their professional well-being was threatened by Jeremiah's singularity. Panicked, they plotted his disgrace. Their "law" and "counsel" and "word" were in danger of being exposed as pious frauds by Jeremiah's honest and passionate life.

The French talk of a *deformation professionelle*—a liability, a tendency to defect, that is inherent in the role one has assumed as say, a physician or a lawyer. The *deformation* to which prophets and priests and wise men are subject is to market God as a commodity, to use God to legitimize self-ishness. It is easy and it is frequent. It happens without deliberate intent.

What I had not foreseen
Was the gradual day
Weakening the will
Leaking the brightness away . . . [9]

A personal name, not an assigned role, is our passbook into reality. It is also our continuing orientation in reality. Any-thing other than our name—title, job description, number, role—is less than a name. Apart from the name that marks us as uniquely created and personally addressed, we slide into fantasies that are out of touch with the world as it is and so we live ineffectively, irresponsibly. Or we live by the stereotypes in which other people cast us that are out of touch with the uniqueness in which God has created us, and so live diminished into boredom, the brightness leaking away.

Jeremiah—a name linked with the name and action of God. The only thing more significant to Jeremiah than his own being was God's being. He fought in the name of the Lord and explored the reality of God and in the process grew and developed, ripened and matured. He was always reaching out, always finding more truth, getting in touch with more of God, becoming more himself, more human.

3 Before

*Before I formed you in the womb I knew you,
and before you were born I consecrated you;
I appointed you a prophet to the nations.*

Jeremiah 1:5

What science will ever be able to reveal to man the origin, nature and character of that conscious power to will and to love which constitutes his life? It is certainly not our effort, nor the effort of anyone around us, which set that current in motion. And it is certainly not our solicitude, nor that of any friend, which prevents its ebb or controls its turbulence. We can, of course, trace back through generations some of the antecedents of the torrent which bears us along; and we can, by means of certain moral and physical disciplines and stimulations, regularise or enlarge the aperture through which the torrent is released into us. But neither that geography nor those artifices help us in theory or in practice to harness the sources of life. My self is given to me far more than it is formed by me. Man, Scripture says, cannot add a cubit to his stature. Still less can he add a unit to the potential of his love, or accelerate by another unit the fundamental rhythm which regulates the ripening of his mind and heart. In the last resort the profound life, the fontal life, the new-born life, escape our grasp entirely.

Pierre Teilhard de Chardin[1]

I was sitting at the counter of a delicatessen in Brooklyn, eating a pastrami sandwich on Jewish rye and making small talk with the owner. After fifteen minutes or so of desultory conversation, neither of us saying much of interest to the other, he planted himself in front of me, assumed a pose of intense concentration and said, "Don't tell me, you are from . . . let's see . . . you come frommmm . . . Nebraska."

"No," I said, "I come from Montana."

He was disappointed, "I usually don't miss it by that far."

The tempo of the conversation picked up. I learned that he took great pride in his ability to distinguish regional accents. Persons from all over the country, from all over the world, came into his store. He had a good ear. He developed fine skills in locating people's origins by listening to dialectical variations in their speech.

I was flattered to be the object of his curiosity. The only previous interest that I can recall shopkeepers having in me was getting my order straight and making sure I got the price right.

"Whaddal ya' have?"

"Hot pastrami on rye. How much?"

"Buck seventy-five."

The language was informational and utilitarian. When it had done its work it either stopped or digressed into gossip. But for those few moments in that Brooklyn setting, someone listened to my words for something more than information; the man was after *knowledge.* He wanted to know where I came from and what I had experienced that resulted in my pronouncing words just the way I did that day.

I was not reduced to a customer with hunger pangs that could be turned into a profit. I had geographic particularity, linguistic idiosyncrasy. There was more to me than my biological needs and economic potential, and he was interested in it, or at least part of it.

In a journalistic age in which the only things that qualify as attention-getting are the immediate and the extraordinary, I am not used to being approached that way. In a commercial age in which each person is evaluated as an economic unit and time is money, I am not used to such leisurely attentiveness. But only this kind of attention allows me to express the many layers of humanness and the complex significance they have for who I am. Apart from the *before*, the *now* has little meaning. The *now* is only a thin slice of who I am; isolated from the rich deposits of *before*, it cannot be understood.

So biographers search through family archives. So psychiatrists recover repressed memories and ask about childhood impressions. So lovers rummage through the photograph albums for everything and anything about one another, knowing that every detail deepens comprehension and therefore deepens love. The *before* is the root system of the visible *now*. Our lives cannot be read as newspaper reports on current events; they are unabridged novels with character and plot development, each paragraph essential for mature appreciation.

Knowing that the fully developed, passionate humanity of Jeremiah necessarily had a complex and intricate background, we prepare to examine it. But we are brought up short. We are told next to nothing: three bare, unadorned background items—his father's name, Hilkiah; his father's vocation, priest; his place of birth, Anathoth. We want to know more. Without more information how can we gain an adequate understanding of the humanity of Jeremiah? We need to know the social and economic conditions of Anathoth so that we can trace the early influences on Jeremiah's passion for justice. We need to know whether the father was passive or assertive in order to evaluate the son's complex emotional life. We need to know if the mother was overly protective and when she weaned her son if we are to account for the incredible tenacity in the adult prophet. We need to know the teaching methods used by local wise men to distinguish between the original and conventional in Jeremiah's preaching and teaching. The questions pile up. Lack of evidence frustrates us. What we need is a breakthrough manuscript discovery in seventh century B.C. Anathoth, manuscripts containing anecdotes, statistics and letters—raw material for a reconstruction of the world into which Jeremiah was born.

We fantasize an archaeological scoop. Meanwhile what we have right before us turns out to be far more useful—a theological probe. Instead of being told what Jeremiah's parents were doing, we are told what his God was doing: "Before I formed you in the womb I knew you, and before you were born I consecrated you; I appointed you a prophet to the nations" (Jer 1:5).

The First Move
Before Jeremiah knew God, God knew Jeremiah: "Before I formed you in the womb I knew you." This turns everything we ever thought about God around. We think that God is an object about which we have questions. We are curious about God. We make inquiries about God. We read books about God. We get into late night bull sessions about God. We drop into church from time to time to see what is going on with God. We indulge in an occasional sunset or symphony to cultivate a feeling of reverence for God.

But that is not the reality of our lives with God. Long before we ever got around to asking questions about God, God has been questioning us. Long before we got inter-

ested in the subject of God, God subjected us to the most
intensive and searching knowledge. Before it ever crossed
our minds that God might be important, God singled us out
as important. Before we were formed in the womb, God
knew us. We are known before we know.

This realization has a practical result: no longer do we
run here and there, panicked and anxious, searching for
the answers to life. Our lives are not puzzles to be figured
out. Rather, we come to God, who knows us and reveals
to us the truth of our lives. The fundamental mistake is to
begin with ourselves and not God. God is the center from
which all life develops. If we use our ego as the center from
which to plot the geometry of our lives, we will live eccentri-
cally.

All wise reflection corroborates Scripture here. We enter
a world we didn't create. We grow into a life already provided for us. We arrive in a complex of relationships with
other wills and destinies that are already in full operation
before we are introduced. If we are going to live appro-
priately, we must be aware that we are living in the middle
of a story that was begun and will be concluded by another.
And this other is God.

My identity does not begin when I begin to understand
myself. There is something previous to what I think about
myself, and it is what God thinks of me. That means that
everything I think and feel is by nature a response, and the
one to whom I respond is God. I never speak the first
word. I never make the first move.

Jeremiah's life didn't start with Jeremiah. Jeremiah's salvation didn't start with Jeremiah. Jeremiah's truth didn't
start with Jeremiah. He entered the world in which the
essential parts of his existence were already ancient history.
So do we.

Sometimes when we are in close and involved conversation with three or four other people, another person joins

the group and abruptly begins saying things, arguing positions and asking questions in complete ignorance of what has been said for the past two hours, oblivious to the delicate conversational balances that have been achieved. When that happens, I always want to say, "Just shut up for a while, won't you? Just sit and listen until you get caught up on what is going on here. Get in tune with what is taking place, then we will welcome you into our conversation."

God is more patient. He puts up with our interruptions; he backtracks and fills us in on the old stories; he repeats the vital information. But how much better it is if we take the time to get the drift of things, to find out where we fit. The story into which life fits is already well on its way when we walk into the room. It is an exciting, brilliant, multivoiced conversation. The smart thing is to find out the identity behind the voices and become familiar with the context in which the words are being used. Then, gradually, we venture a statement, make a reflection, ask a question or two, even dare to register an objection. It is not long before we are regular participants in the conversation in which, as it unfolds, we get to know ourselves even as we are known.

Choosing Sides
The second item of background information provided on Jeremiah is this: "Before you were born I consecrated you." *Consecrated* means set apart for God's side. It means that the human is not a cogwheel. It means that a person is not the keyboard of a piano on which circumstances play hit-parade tunes.[2] It means we are chosen out of the feckless stream of circumstantiality for something important that God is doing.

What is God doing? He is saving; he is rescuing; he is blessing; he is providing; he is judging; he is healing; he is enlightening. There is a spiritual war in progress, an all-out moral battle. There is evil and cruelty, unhappiness and illness. There is superstition and ignorance, brutality and pain. God is in continuous and energetic battle against all of it. God is for life and against death. God is for love and against hate. God is for hope and against despair. God is for heaven and against hell. There is no neutral ground in the universe. Every square foot of space is contested.

Jeremiah, before he was born, was enlisted on God's side in this war. He wasn't given a few years in which to look around and make up his mind which side he would be on, or even whether he would join a side at all. He was already chosen as a combatant on God's side. And so are we all. No one enters existence as a spectator. We either take up the life to which we have been consecrated or we traitorously defect from it. We cannot say, "Hold it! I am not quite ready. Wait until I have sorted things out."[3]

For a long time all Christians called each other "saints." They were all saints regardless of how well or badly they lived, of how experienced or inexperienced they were. The word *saint* did not refer to the quality or virtue of their acts, but to the kind of life to which they had been chosen, life on a battlefield. It was not a title given after a spectacular performance, but a mark of whose side they were on. The word *saint* is the noun form of the verb *consecrated* that gave spiritual shape to Jeremiah even before he had biological shape.

In the neighborhood in which I lived when I was in the first grade all the children were older than I. When we had neighborhood games and chose up sides, I was always the last one chosen. There was one time—it probably happened more than once, but this once sticks in my memory—that when everyone else had been chosen, I was left standing in the middle between the two teams. The captains argued over who was going to have to choose me. Having me, I suddenly realized, was a liability. As the argument raged between them I went from being a zero to a minus.

But not with God. Not a zero. Not a minus. I have a set-apart place that only I can fill. No one can substitute for me. No one can replace me. Before I was good for anything, God decided that I was good for what he was doing. My place in life doesn't depend on how well I do in the entrance examination. My place in life is not determined by what market there is for my type of personality.

God is out to win the world in love and each person has been selected in the same way that Jeremiah was, to be set apart to do it with him. He doesn't wait to see how we turn out to decide to choose or not to choose us. Before we were born he chose us for his side—consecrated us.

The Great Giveaway
The third thing that God did to Jeremiah before Jeremiah did anything on his own was this: "I appointed you a prophet to the nations." The word *appointed* is, literally, "gave" *(nathan)*—I *gave* you as a prophet to the nations. God gives. He is generous. He is lavishly generous. Before Jeremiah ever got it together he was given away.

That is God's way. He did it with his own son, Jesus. He gave him away. He gave him to the nations. He did not keep him on display. He did not preserve him in a museum. He did not show him off as a trophy. "God so loved the world that he gave his only Son, that whoever believes in him should not perish but have eternal life" (Jn 3:16).

And he gave Jeremiah away. I can hear Jeremiah objecting, "Wait a minute. Don't be so quick to give me away. I've got something to say about this. I've got my inalienable rights. I have a few decisions about life that I am going to make myself." Imagine God's response: "Sorry, but I did it before you were even born. It's already done; you are given away."

Some things we have a choice in, some we don't. In this we don't. It is **the** kind of world into which we were born.

God created it. God sustains it. Giving is the style of the universe. Giving is woven into the fabric of existence. If we try to live by getting instead of giving, we are going against the grain. It is like trying to go against the law of gravity—the consequence is bruises and broken bones. In fact, we do see a lot of distorted, misshapen, crippled lives among those who defy the reality that all life is given and must continue to be given to be true to its nature.

There is a rocky cliff on the shoreline of the Montana lake where I live part of each summer. There are breaks in the rock face in which tree swallows make their nests. For several weeks one summer I watched the swallows in swift flight collect insects barely above the surface of the water then dive into the cavities in the cliff, feeding first their mates and then their new-hatched chicks. Near one of the cracks in the cliff face a dead branch stretched about four feet over the water. One day I was delighted to see three new swallows sitting side by side on this branch. The parents made wide, sweeping, insect-gathering circuits over the water and then returned to the enormous cavities that those little birds became as they opened their beaks for a feeding.

This went on for a couple of hours until the parents decided they had had enough of it. One adult swallow got alongside the chicks and started shoving them out toward the end of the branch—pushing, pushing, pushing. The end one fell off. Somewhere between the branch and the water four feet below, the wings started working, and the fledgling was off on his own. Then the second one. The third was not to be bullied. At the last possible moment his grip on the branch loosened just enough so that he swung downward, then tightened again, bulldog tenacious. The parent was without sentiment. He pecked at the desperately clinging talons until it was more painful for the poor chick to hang on than risk the insecurities of flying. The grip was released and the inexperienced wings began pumping. The mature swallow knew what the chick did not—that it would fly—that there was no danger in making it do what it was perfectly designed to do.

Birds have feet and can walk. Birds have talons and can grasp a branch securely. They can walk; they can cling. But *flying* is their characteristic action, and not until they fly are they living at their best, gracefully and beautifully.

Giving is what we do best. It is the air into which we were born. It is the action that was designed into us before our birth. *Giving* is the way the world is. God gives himself. He also gives away everything that is. He makes no exceptions for any of us. We are given away to our families, to our neighbors, to our friends, to our enemies—to the nations. Our life is for others. That is the way creation works. Some of us try desperately to hold on to ourselves, to live for ourselves. We look so bedraggled and pathetic doing it, hanging on to the dead branch of a bank account for dear life, afraid to risk ourselves on the untried wings of giving. We don't think we can live generously because we have never tried. But the sooner we start the better, for we are going to have to give up our lives finally, and the longer we wait the less time we have for the soaring and swooping life of grace.

Jeremiah could have hung on to the dead-end street where he was born in Anathoth. He could have huddled in the security of his father's priesthood. He could have conformed to the dull habits of his culture. He didn't. He believed what had been told him about his background, that God long before gave him away, and he participated in the giving, throwing himself into his appointment.

Dignity and Design
Many critical things happen before I am conceived and born that predetermine the reality that I experience: biological things that make me a biped that walks and not a fish that swims, geographic things that provide me a tem-

perate zone instead of an ice age, scientific things that produce physicians to visit when I am sick and not witch-doctors, political things that make me a citizen in a democracy and not a serf on a feudal estate. But the most important things are what God did before I was conceived, before I was born. He knew me, therefore I am no accident; he chose me, therefore I cannot be a zero; he gave me, therefore I must not be a consumer.

There are frenzied efforts in our culture to salvage ruined self-esteem by bolstering people with reassurance and affirmation, by telling them that they are terrific, that they are number one, and that they had better treat themselves to a good time. The result is not larger persons but smaller ones —pygmy egos. But how do we acquire a sense of significance without puffing up the ego? How do we become important without becoming self-important, confident without being arrogant, dignified without looking ridiculous?

Jeremiah sets the pattern. Has anyone lived so well out of such deep reservoirs of dignity and design—no hollow piece of strutting straw!—as Jeremiah? He did it from a base of meditation on the awesome *before* of his life, and he lived *out of* this background and not *against* it. This, not Anathoth, was where he came from, and the accent in his speech betrays his origins to anyone with a sensitive ear.

It is difficult to cultivate this kind of depth-memory awareness. We get no help from our contemporaries who rarely go back further than the minutes of the previous meeting in an attempt to understand the agenda of their humanity. We are so used to considering everything through the prism of our current feelings and our most recent acquisitions that it is a radical change to consider the vast *before*. But if we would live well, it is necessary. Otherwise we live feebly and gropingly, blind to the glory that we are known, chosen and given away by God.

4 I Am Only a Youth

Then I said, "Ah, Lord GOD! Behold, I do not know how
to speak, for I am only a youth." But the LORD said to me,
"Do not say, 'I am only a youth';
for to all to whom I send you you shall go,
and whatever I command you you shall speak.
Be not afraid of them,
for I am with you to deliver you, says the LORD. . . .
Behold, I make you this day a fortified city, an iron pillar,
and bronze walls, against the whole land, against the kings of
Judah, its princes, its priests, and the people of the land."

Jeremiah 1:6-8, 18

"I am not made for perilous quests," cried Frodo.
I wish I had never seen the Ring! Why did it come to
me? Why was I chosen?"

"Such questions cannot be answered," said Gandalf.
"You may be sure that it was not for any merit that
others do not possess; not for power or wisdom, at any
rate. But you have been chosen and you must therefore
use such strength and heart and wits as you have."

J. R. R. Tolkien[1]

God asked Jeremiah to do something he couldn't do. Naturally, he refused. If we are asked to do something that we know that we cannot do, it is foolish to accept the assignment, for it soon becomes an embarrassment to everyone.

The job Jeremiah refused was to be a prophet. There are two interlaced convictions that characterize a prophet. The first conviction is that God is personal and alive and active. The second conviction is that what is going on right now, in this world at this time in history, is critical. A prophet is obsessed with *God*, and a prophet is immersed in the *now*. God is as real to a prophet as his next-door neighbor, and his next-door neighbor is a vortex in which God's purposes are being worked out.

The work of the prophet is to call people to live well, to live rightly—to be human. But it is more than a call to say something, it is a call to live out the message. The prophet must be what he or she says. The person as well as the message of the prophet challenges us to live up to our creation, to live into our salvation—to become all that we are designed to be.

We cannot be human if we are not in relation to God. We can be an animal and be unaware of God. We can be an aggregate of minerals and be unaware of God. But humanity requires relationship with God before it can be itself. "As the scholastics used to say: *Homo non proprie humanus sed superhumanus est*—which means that to be properly human, you must go beyond the merely human."[2]

A relationship with God is not something added on after we complete our basic growth, it is the essential core of that growth. Take that core out, and there is no humanity at all but only a husk, the appearance but not the substance of the human. Nor can we be human if we are not existing in the present, for the present is where God meets us. If we avoid the details of the actual present, we abdicate a big chunk of our humanity. Søren Kierkegaard parodies our inattentiveness to our immediate reality when he writes about the man who was caught up in things and projects and causes so abstracted from himself that he woke up one day and found himself dead.[3]

A prophet lets people know who God is and what he is like, what he says, and what he is doing. A prophet wakes us up from our sleepy complacency so that we see the great and stunning drama that is our existence, and then pushes us onto the stage playing our parts whether we think we are ready or not. A prophet angers us by rejecting our euphemisms and ripping off our disguises, then dragging our heartless attitudes and selfish motives out into the open where everyone sees them for what they are. A prophet makes everything and everyone seem significant and important—important because God made it, or him, or her; significant because God is actively, right now, using it, or him, or her. A prophet makes it difficult to continue with a sloppy or selfish life.

Pleading Inadequacy

No job is more important, for what is more important than a persuasive presentation of the invisible but living reality, God? And what is more important than a convincing demonstration of the eternal meaning of the visible, ordinary stuff of daily life? But important or not, Jeremiah refused. He was not qualified. He had not done well in the God courses in school. And he hadn't been around long enough to know how the world works. "Ah, Lord GOD! Behold, I do not know how to speak, for I am only a youth."

We are practiced in pleading inadequacy in order to avoid living at the best that God calls us to. How tired the excuses sound! I am only a youth; I am only a housewife; I am only a layman; I am only a poor preacher; I only have an eighth-grade education; I don't have enough time; I don't have enough training; I don't have enough confidence; or, with biblical precedence, "Oh, my Lord, I am not eloquent" (Ex 4:10). Too much is being asked of us. We cannot cope. We cannot manage.

If we look at ourselves and are absolutely honest, we are always inadequate. Of course, we are not always honest. We fudge and cheat on the tests. We cover up a bit here; we bluff a bit there. We pretend to be more sure than we are.

Our race would not have gotten far,
Had we not learned to bluff it out
And look more certain than we are
Of what our motion is about.[4]

Life, in fact, *is* too much for us. This business of living in awareness and response to God, in attentive love to the people with us, and in reverent appreciation of the world round about exceeds our capacities. We aren't smart enough; we don't have enough energy; we can't concentrate adequately. We are apathetic, slouching and slovenly. Not all the time, to be sure. We have spurts of love, passionate risks of faith, impressive episodes of courageous caring. But then we slip back into indolence or greed. Soon we are back at the old stand, handing out the glib patter that fools others into thinking we are better than we really are. Sometimes we even deceive ourselves into thinking we are pretty nice people indeed. Jeremiah knew it all from the inside: "the heart is deceitful above all things, and desperately corrupt" (Jer 17:9).

But a ruthless honesty will always leave us shattered by our inadequacy. The world is a frightening place. If we are not a little bit scared, we simply don't know what is going on. If we are pleased with ourselves, we either don't have very high standards or have amnesia in regard to the central reality, for "it is a fearful thing to fall into the hands of the living God" (Heb 10:31). Pascal said, "Fear not, provided you fear; but if you fear not, then fear."[5]

There is an enormous gap between what we think we can do and what God calls us to do. Our ideas of what we can do or want to do are trivial; God's ideas for us are grand. God's call to Jeremiah to be a prophet parallels his call to us to be a person. The excuses we make are plausible; often they are statements of fact, but they are excuses all the same and are disallowed by our Lord, who says: "Do not say, 'I am only a youth'; for to all to whom I send you you shall go, and whatever I command you you shall speak. Be not afraid of them, for I am with you to deliver you, says the LORD." The Lord then put forth his hand and touched Jeremiah's mouth, saying, "Behold, I have put my words in your mouth. See, I have set you this day over nations and over kingdoms, to pluck up and to break down, to destroy and to overthrow, to build and to plant" (Jer 1:9-10).

The three pairs of verbs (*pluck up/break down, destroy/ overthrow, build/plant*) are all-involving. In the way of faith we do not escape because it is too much for us; we plunge into it because we are commanded and equipped. It is not our feelings that determine our level of participation in life, nor our experience that qualifies us for what we will do and be; it is what God decides about us. God does not send us into the dangerous and exacting life of faith because we are qualified; he chooses us in order to qualify us for what he wants us to be and do: "I have put my words in your mouth. . . . I have set you this day over nations."

Eight verses down the page Jeremiah is no longer inadequate. "And I, behold, I make you this day a fortified city, an iron pillar, and bronze walls, against the whole land, against the kings of Judah, its princes, its priests, and the people of the land. They will fight against you; but they shall not prevail against you, for I am with you, says the LORD, to deliver you" (Jer 1:18-19). Everything that we know about Jeremiah shows that this in fact happened. In a forty-year public ministry through the most confused and chaotic decades of Israel's entire history, Jeremiah was invincible. Inwardly he was in great agony many times, but he never swerved from his course. He was mocked cruelly and persecuted severely, but he never deviated from his position. There was enormous pressure on him to change, to compromise, to quit and to hide. He never did it. He was "bronze walls."

How did Jeremiah make the transition from the shuffling, excuse-making "Ah, LORD, I am only a youth" to the "iron pillar" career of accepting the assignment as prophet? God equipped Jeremiah for life by showing him two visions. The two visions led Jeremiah from enervating inadequacy to adrenalin-charged obedience.

A Rod of Almond

The first vision was of a rod of almond: " 'Jeremiah, what do you see?' And I said, 'I see a rod of almond.' Then the LORD said to me, 'You have seen well, for I am watching over my word to perform it' " (Jer 1:11-12).

The almond tree is one of the earliest trees to bloom in Palestine. Before it puts forth leaves, it puts forth blossoms, white and snowy. While the land is still chill from winter, the warm blossoms, untended and unforced, surprise us with a promise of spring. Every spring it happens again: the explosion of blossom in our forests and gardens before the leaves are out, before the grass is green. And we know what is coming next: migratory birds will soon be filling the air with song; leaves will festoon the trees with great banners of green; fruit will begin to develop. The blossom is a delight in itself, beautiful to look at, fragrant to smell. But it is more. It is anticipation. It is promise. Like words. "I am watching over my word to perform it." Words, like the almond blossom, are promises, anticipations of what is about to take place. They *become* something. "The word *became* flesh."

The vision is accented with a word play. The word *almond* and the word *watching* are nearly identical in Hebrew. "What do you see, Jeremiah?" I see a *shaqed* ("almond"). "Good! you see very well, for I am *shoqed* ("watching") my word to perform it. I am watching my word like a shepherd watching his flock. Not one of these words that you hear me speak will wander off. Not one will be lost. I'll bring each word to some kind of living completion."

The method was audio-visual: a visual image joined to an auditory pun trained Jeremiah in hope. Every spring for the rest of his life the sight of the almond blossom, *shaqed*, would trigger the sound *shoqed* ("watching") in his memory ("I am watching over my word to perform it"), and for the rest of his life every time he heard the everyday word *shoqed* ("watching") spoken—and there could not have been many days when he did not—the visual image of the *shaqed* ("almond") would release all the life-enhancing, energy-releasing associations of spring.

There is no living the life of faith, whether by prophet or person, without some kind of sustaining vision like this. At some deep level we need to be convinced, and in some way or other we need periodic reminders, that no words are mere words. In particular, God's words are not mere words. They are promises that lead to fulfillments. God performs what he announces. God does what he says.

A Boiling Pot
The second vision was of a boiling pot: " 'What do you see?' And I said, 'I see a boiling pot, facing away from the north' " (Jer 1:13). The pot was tipped so that the scalding water was being spilled to the south. The village of Anathoth and the Jerusalem streets and courtyards were directly in the path of its flow.

The boiling water cascading down toward Israel is identified as enemy armies poised for an invasion (Jer 1:14-16).
The nations to the north were boiling a kettle of war that
was going to inundate the land with evil—murder and rape
and pillage. The seething turbulence on the horizon was
going to spill over into the pleasant hills of Judea. The
enemy kings and officers, audacious and mocking, would
camp right in front of the city gates and around the city
walls. This imminent war is linked with God's judgment.
The boiling water is going to wash the land. "I believe in
getting into hot water," said G. K. Chesterton, "it keeps you
clean."[6] The scalding judgment was coming because the
people had abandoned a relationship of love with God and
taken up with little religious rituals and picayune idolatries
(Jer 1:16). The war would interrupt their inane and distracted, their soiled and silly lives and force them to attend
to what is essential and eternal: life and death, God and
humanity, faith and faithfulness, covenant and obedience.

The subject of the vision is negative (in contrast to the
almond vision) but its message is positive, for its effect is
to *contain* evil. The boiling pot is a container, located at a
specific place on the compass.

Neither Jeremiah nor the people needed a vision to tell
them that danger was gathering momentum in the north.
Everybody knew that.[7] The Neo-Babylonian armies were
on the move and no reasonably intelligent person could fail
to be aware of it. It did, though, take a vision to see that the
evil had limits. The boiling-pot vision named, located and
limited the evil that was afflicting everyone with a kind of
metaphysical paranoia.

Uninstructed and untrained we let evil seep through the
atmosphere and through our emotions like a fog, obscur-
ing the sharp outlines of reality and absorbing everything
in its ominous, soggy gray. In such an atmosphere we are
terrorized by every rumor, jumpy at every noise, edgy and

anxious. It is certainly true that there is evil in the world—
a great deal of it. And it is frightening. If we live realistically,
with our eyes open, we see a lot of evil. Seeing all that evil,
how can we relax? How can we engage in such undramatic
counteractions as giving cups of cold water to thirsty strangers? The vision supplies the answer: the evil is not everything, and it is not everywhere. It is named. It has an origin
and a finish. The evil that has its paralyzing grip on everyone is not a wild, uncontrollable evil; it is a carefully commanded judgment, with God as the commander. The boiling pot reduces evil to a location and a use. We cannot af-
ford to be naive about evil—it must be faced. But we cannot
be intimidated by it either. It will be used by God to bring
good. For it is one of the most extraordinary aspects of the
good news that God uses bad men to accomplish his good
purposes. The great paradox of judgment is that evil becomes fuel in the furnace of salvation.

Uninstructed by this vision, or something like it, we lose
our sense of proportion and are incapacitated for living in
open and adventurous response to whatever comes to us
through the day. If we forget that the newspapers are foot-
notes to Scripture and not the other way around, we will
finally be afraid to get out of bed in the morning. Too many
of us spend far too much time with the editorial page and
not nearly enough with the prophetic vision. We get our
interpretation of politics and economics and morals from
journalists when we should be getting only information; the
meaning of the world is most accurately given to us by God's
Word.

The two visions, the blossoming almond branch and the
pot of boiling water, were Jeremiah's Harvard and Yale.
The single-image visions burned themselves deep into the
retina of his faith. By means of these visions he kept his
balance and sanity and passion in the theater of God's glory
and through the holocaust of human sin. Whether he was

ecstatic in the splendor or nauseated by the stench of evil, he kept his grip on reality, never retreating into a cave of self-pity, never shutting his eyes to the ugly evil around him, never cynically dismissive of the glory exploding around him.

The first vision convinced Jeremiah that the word of God bursts with wonders and that its wonders are not illusions. The second vision convinced Jeremiah that the world is very dangerous but that the danger is not catastrophic.

In order to be equipped to be what God calls us to be—prophet, person—and not be crippled all our lives by inadequacy, we need to know supremely these two subjects, God and world, and to be trained in them thoroughly. In both subjects first impressions and surface appearances are deceiving. We underestimate God and we overestimate evil. We don't see what God is doing and conclude that he is doing nothing. We see everything that evil is doing and think it is in control of everyone. The visions penetrate appearances. By means of the blossoming almond and the boiling pot we are trained to live with a keen edge of hope and to never be intimidated by evil. For if we are going to live in God's image, alive to all that is God, open and responsive to all he is doing, we must trust in his word, trust what we do not see. And if we are going to live in the world, attentive to each particularity, loving it through all the bad times without being repelled by it or afraid of it or conformed to it, we are going to have to face its immense evil, but know at the same time that it is a limited and controlled evil.

Vision-Shaped
Did the visions work? Do they? Jeremiah's life is evidence that the visions were the educational curriculum that directed development from an insecure youth to a solid, mature adult. Jeremiah was shaped by the visions, not by the

fashions of the day, not by his feelings about himself. We know that he often felt terrible and that he was treated terribly. He often felt weak; he often was near despair. In fact, he was always strong. His emotions often failed him; his faith always held fast.

His strength was not achieved by growing calluses over his highly sensitive spirit. Throughout his life Jeremiah experienced an astonishing range of emotions. His spirit registered, it seems, everything. He was one of those finely tuned persons who pick up and respond to the slightest tremors around him. At the same time he was utterly impervious to assault and mockery, to persecution and opposition.

The thorough integration of strength and sensitivity, of firmness and feeling, is rare. We sometimes see sensitive people who are unstrung most of the time. They bleed profusely at the sight of blood. Their sensitivity incapacitates them for action in the rough-and-tumble cruelties of the world. In contrast others are rigid moralists, ramrod stiff with righteous rectitude. There is never any doubt about their dogmatically asserted position. But their principles are hammers that crack skulls and bruise flesh. The world makes a wide circuit around such persons. It is dangerous to be in their company for very long, for if they detect any mental weakness or moral wavering in us, we will be lucky to escape without at least a headache.

But not Jeremiah. Educated by the almond rod, his inward responsiveness to the personal, whether God or human, deepened and developed. Educated by the boiling pot, his outward capacity to deal with dehumanizing evil and to resist depersonalizing intimidation became invincible: "a fortified city, an iron pillar, bronze walls." Not bad for someone who started out as "only a youth."

5 Do Not Trust in These Deceptive Words

The word that came to Jeremiah from the LORD: "Stand in the gate of the LORD's house, and proclaim there this word, and say, Hear the word of the LORD, all you men of Judah who enter these gates to worship the LORD. Thus says the LORD of hosts, the God of Israel, Amend your ways and your doings, and I will let you dwell in this place. Do not trust in these deceptive words: 'This is the temple of the LORD, the temple of the LORD, the temple of the LORD.' "

Jeremiah 7:1-4

Jesus today has many who love his heavenly kingdom, but few who carry his cross; many who yearn for comfort, few who long for distress. Plenty of people he finds to share his banquet, few to share his fast. Everyone desires to take part in his rejoicing, but few are willing to suffer anything for his sake. There are many that follow Jesus as far as the breaking of bread, few as far as drinking the cup of suffering; many that revere his miracles, few that follow him in the indignity of his cross.

Thomas à Kempis[1]

Manasseh was the worst king the Hebrews ever had. He was a thoroughly bad man presiding over a totally corrupt government. He reigned in Jerusalem for fifty-five years, a dark and evil half century.

He encouraged a pagan worship that involved whole communities in sexual orgies. He installed cult prostitutes at shrines throughout the countryside. He imported wizards and sorcerers who enslaved the people in superstitions and manipulated them with their magic. The man could not do enough evil. There seemed to be no end to his barbarous cruelties. His capacity for inventing new forms of evil seemed bottomless. His appetite for the sordid was insatiable. One day he placed his son on the altar in some black and terrible ritual of witchcraft and burned him as an offering (2 Kings 21).

The great Solomonic temple in Jerusalem, resplendent in its holy simplicity, empty of any form of god so that the invisible God could be attended to in worship, swarmed with magicians and prostitutes. Idols shaped as beasts and monsters defiled the holy place. Lust and greed were deified. Murders were commonplace. Manasseh dragged the people into a mire far more stinking than anything the world had yet seen. The sacred historian's judgment was blunt: "Manasseh seduced them to do more evil than the nations had done whom the LORD destroyed before the people of Israel" (2 Kings 21:9).[2]

Jeremiah was born in the last decade of Manasseh's rule. This is the world in which Jeremiah learned to walk and talk and play. No worse environment in which to raise a child can be imagined. It was a slum society: "On every side the wicked prowl, as vileness is exalted among the sons of men" (Ps 12:8).

Fifty-five years of such misrule brought the faith close to oblivion. Some old people remembered prophetic oracles and acts of true worship. Rumors of holiness were no doubt whispered about. Hidden pockets of faithful people maintained a fugitive existence. Then Manasseh died. His son Amon succeeded him. The people watched to see if things would change. They didn't. The evil continued. But the people had their stomachs full. They had reached the breaking point and could take no more. Amon was murdered. His eight-year-old son, Josiah, was put on the throne.

Josiah's Reforms

Now begins one of the most remarkable chapters in the story of these people who are our ancestors. Somehow in this boy king there was an innocence and uncorrupt spirit that God was able to use to bring new life to the land.

We wonder how Josiah got started, for he had no models to work from. Goodness originates at some deep level inaccessible to our investigations. When I see a large expanse of black asphalt parking lot, I sometimes think of Manasseh and Josiah. The asphalt is ugly and forbidding. A fresh green creation has been bulldozed into oblivion to make way for this sterile, monotonous surface. A harsh and brutal technology has obliterated a delicately nuanced life for the convenience of the worshipers of the god Mammon. But before long, cracks appear and grasses, wildflowers, even sprouting trees, push their way through. The underground forces of life break through the surface patina of death. Maintenance engineers patch and fill and seal to keep their surface intact and smooth. If they are inattentive for so much as a season or two, seemingly fragile but in fact formidable life reasserts itself.

I speak of the unremarked
Forces that split the heart
And make the pavement toss—

Forces concealed in quiet
People and plants...[3]

Mannasseh had covered the Holy Land with sodom-and-gomorrah asphalt. But the holy was not gone, only invisible. Josiah was one of the first shoots to break through the black bitumen. Out of some deep, intuitive longing for God that corrupt parents had not been able to quash, that an evil environment had not been able to annihilate, he asked questions: How could a better rule be established? What could he do as king to recover health and goodness in the garbage dump that was Jerusalem? He had to start some place. He started at the place of worship.

A people's lives are only as good as their worship. The temple in Jerusalem was the architectural evidence of the importance of God in the life of the people. All the lines of life crisscrossed in the temple. Meaning was established there. Values were created there. Worship defines life. If worship is corrupt, life will be corrupt. For fifty-seven years lust and violence in the temple had percolated into the streets and homes and villages of the nation. Josiah began by cleaning up the temple.

As the temple was being renovated and repaired, Hilkiah the priest found an old book there. The book was brought to Josiah and read aloud to him. It was the book of Deuteronomy. Imagine the impact of that reading. Here is Josiah, disgusted with the evil of his father and grandfather and determined to do something about it, but not knowing quite how. He had no blueprint, no direction, no counsel. The only thing he had inherited from his father and grandfather was fifty-seven years of evil. Now he had this powerful document about the love of God and our worship of him, clear definitions of what is right and wrong, and explicit directions on how to make moral decisions and conduct intelligent worship. In Josiah's ears the reading was "a thunderclap of conscience."[4]

The young king's response was swift and commanding. He immediately put into action everything that he read. Now that he knew what true worship was, he banished every vestige of false worship. The government-subsidized immorality was wiped out. The cult prostitutes who had special housing in the temple were turned out. The magicians and sorcerers who had set up shop in the temple precincts were scattered. Josiah dispersed his agents throughout the land announcing what was discovered in this scroll. Old altars were torn down and people were taught the way of faith. It was exciting, dramatic and glorious. "Never had there been a reform so sweeping in its aims and so consistent in execution!"[5]

The muck of a half century of corruption was shoveled out of the city, out of the land. The place had been a religious zoo. At the old places of worship you could get any loathsome desire gratified, any murderous ambition licensed. There was a ritual and god or goddess for every whim. Under Manasseh religion was centered in what William James, in a memorable phrase, called the "convulsive little ego."[6] Religion was supernatural assistance to do whatever you wished: make money, insure a good harvest, feel good, murder the person you hate, get ahead of your neighbor. Now, under Josiah, religion centered in one holy God. Religion became what it must be but often is not—a way of discovering the meaning of life, of ordering justice in society, of finding direction toward goals of excellence, of acquiring the discipline to live with integrity, of realizing how God loves and of learning how to love God in return.

A Ringside Seat

Jeremiah had a ringside seat in the arena of this reform. It is hardly conceivable though that he remained a spectator. He was not the sort of person to stand on the sidelines. He helped. He participated in the reform with his preaching.

We have fragments of his sermons.

"You have polluted the land," he said, "with your vile harlotry" (Jer 3:2). The people had abandoned the God who loved and called them into being and had given themselves in reckless prodigality to every god and goddess they met. Moral pollution works the same way as environmental pollution. The waste products of careless living work insidiously into the soil of thought and the streams of language, poisoning every part of society.

Jeremiah pleaded with them: "Break up your fallow ground" (Jer 4:3). Superstition and idolatry form a tough crust that makes us insensitive and unreceptive to the word that God speaks in mercy and salvation. Ploughing is a metaphor for the repentance that prepares the ground of our hearts to receive what God has for us.

Jeremiah was scathing and sarcastic: "What do you mean that you dress in scarlet . . . that you enlarge your eyes with paint? In vain you beautify yourself" (Jer 4:30). Do you think that by using cosmetics you can change your destiny? It is you yourselves who need to be changed.

Through it all Jeremiah conveyed hope: "Stand by the roads, and look, and ask for the ancient paths, where the good way is; and walk in it, and find rest for your souls" (Jer 6:16). There *are* ancient paths, well-trodden and clearly marked, that lead to goodness and to God. The Scriptures—in this case the Deuteronomy scroll—map the roads. If we ignore them, we stumble over obstacles. Jeremiah's preaching was tireless in insisting on the plain, obvious truth: that God is among us, that we can and must live in faithful love with him.

Only Skin-deep Reform
The reform was accomplished. Everything that a king's commands could do was done: conspicuous crime was stopped; superstitious religion was sent packing; immoral

worship was banned. But getting rid of evil does not make people good. It didn't take Jeremiah long to realize that the reform was only skin-deep. Everything had changed, but nothing had changed. The outward changes had been enormous; the inward changes were imperceptible.

It isn't long before we find Jeremiah standing in the gates of the Jerusalem temple preaching an odd sermon. This is the very temple that had been the focus for the impressive and successful reform. We would expect a note of congratulation, praising the people for cleaning up the place, getting rid of the wizards, banishing the cult prostitutes, making it safe to walk the street again without getting mugged or murdered. But we hear nothing like that. Everybody is coming to church, arriving at the temple to offer sacrifices just as they are commanded to do in the new best-selling book of Deuteronomy. Worship of the Lord is popular and enthusiastic. The throngs were euphoric: "This is the temple of the LORD, the temple of the LORD, the temple of the LORD."

And what is Jeremiah saying? This: "Do not trust in these deceptive words: 'This is the temple of the LORD, the temple of the LORD, the temple of the LORD.' " The people stood in the holy place and spoke the current religious cliché and supposed that everything was just fine. They were in the right place, and they said the right words—but *they* were not right. The reform was necessary, but it was not enough. For religion is not a matter of arrangements or places or words, but of life and love, of mercy and obedience, of persons in a passion of faith.

Just when Jeremiah expected the people, free from the corruption of Manasseh, to launch into a life of faith using their energy in love, venturing into justice and peace, he arrives at the temple, and what does he find? He finds the people stupidly pleased with themselves and repeating the reform slogan "temple of the LORD, temple of the

LORD, temple of the LORD." Jeremiah is irate.

Places are important—immensely important. Sites and buildings are places where we gather ourselves for fresh action and assemble ourselves for new endeavor. But standing in a church singing a hymn doesn't make us holy any more than standing in a barn and neighing makes us a horse.

And words are important—immensely important. What we say and the way we say it expresses what is most personal and intimate in us. But mindlessly repeating holy words no more creates a relationship than saying "I love you" twenty times a day makes us skilled lovers.

Only because the reform was successful could this kind of thing happen. The temple was now clearly the Lord's temple and not a pagan shrine. When the people came they did not buy amulets, or visit the cult prostitute, or pay to get their fortune told—they worshiped the way they had been commanded by Moses. They were in the right place, saying the right thing. Yet Jeremiah calls their presence and the words there a lie.

Born Again, Born Again, Born Again

This sermon by Jeremiah is so important to us. It is especially important in times of success, when everything is going well, when the church is admired and church attendance swells. We think everything is fine because the appearances are fine and the statistics are impressive. The church is never in so much danger as when it is popular and millions of people are saying "I'm born again, born again, born again."

Jeremiah is as concerned with the right place and the right words as anyone. He, after all, fought hard for this reform. But the right place and the right words are not the life of faith but only the opportunity for the life of faith. They can just as easily be used as a respectable front for a corrupt self. Jeremiah accused the people of just this, using God's temple as a front for a robber's den (Jer 7:11).

A robber's den is a secure place to hide between forays into the countryside to pillage weak and unprotected travelers. After these raids for plunder the robbers go back to the cave where they are safe. That is Jeremiah's accusation: "You have found a safe place, haven't you! This nice, clean temple. You spend all week out in the world doing what you want to do, taking advantage of others, exploiting the weak, cursing the person who isn't pliable to your plans, and, then you repair to this place where everything is in order and protected and right." Six hundred and fifty years later Jesus used Jeremiah's text in his "spring cleaning" temple sermon (Mk 11:15-19) and Paul similarly warned Timothy of those who were "holding the form of religion but denying the power of it" (2 Tim 3:5).

Jeremiah is specific in his arraignment: "Will you steal, murder, commit adultery, swear falsely, burn incense to Baal, and go after other gods that you have not known, and then come and stand before me in this house, which is called by my name, and say, 'We are delivered!'—only to go on doing all these abominations?" (Jer 7:9-10). Their religious performance was impeccable; their everyday life was rotten.

The outside is a lot easier to reform than the inside. Going to the right church and saying the right words is a lot easier than working out a life of justice and love among the people you work and live with. Showing up at church once a week and saying a hearty Amen is a lot easier than engaging in a life of daily prayer and Scripture meditation that develops into concern for poverty and injustice, hunger and war.

Images without Substance
Are the people who do this deliberately trying to pull the

wool over the eyes of their neighbors and fake God into blessing them? Some are, but for most I don't think so. I don't think they are trying to get by with anything. I think they have lived for so long on the basis of outward appearances that they have no feel for inward reality. I think they were so impressed with the success of the reform that they thought that was all there was to it. We live in a culture where image is everything and substance nothing. We live in a culture where a new beginning is far more attractive than a long follow-through. Images are important. Beginnings are important. But an image without substance is a lie. A beginning without a continuation is a lie.

Jeremiah attempted to shock his people into a recognition of this obvious but avoided truth by sending them on a field trip to Shiloh: "Go now to my place that was in Shiloh, where I made my name dwell at first, and see what I did to it for the wickedness of my people Israel" (Jer 7:12).

Shiloh was one of the most famous holy places in Hebrew history. Located at the center of the country, it had been the earliest focus for worship and consultation in Israel. When Joshua brought the people into the land after their deliverance from Egypt and forty years of wilderness wandering, Shiloh was where they assembled, set up the tabernacle and divided up the land among the twelve tribes. The revered ark of the covenant was kept at Shiloh. The great prophet Samuel spoke his words of counsel there. Shiloh was a magnificent beginning. Shiloh was a glorious image. But all Shiloh was now was a few piles of rocks in a field of weeds, as every traveler from Galilee to Jerusalem could see. Shiloh was the right place; at Shiloh the right words were spoken. But when the right place no longer launched a walk with God and when the right words no longer expressed love and faith, Shiloh was destroyed.

If it could happen to Shiloh, it can happen to Jerusalem —and any other place where people gather to worship God.

It is not enough to be in the right place; it is not enough to say the right words; it is never enough until we are walking with God twenty-four hours a day everywhere we go, with everything we say an expression of love and faith.

A Lifelong Career

When I talk with people who come to me in preparation for marriage I often say, "Weddings are easy; marriages are difficult." The couple want to plan a wedding; I want to plan a marriage. They want to know where the bridesmaids will stand; I want to develop a plan for forgiveness. They want to discuss the music of the wedding; I want to talk about the emotions of the marriage. I can do a wedding in twenty minutes with my eyes shut; a marriage takes year after year after year of alert, wide-eyed attention.

Weddings are important. They are beautiful; they are impressive; they are emotional; sometimes they are expensive. We weep at weddings and we laugh at weddings. We take care to be at the right place at the right time and say the right words. Where people stand is important. The way people dress is significant. Every detail—this flower, that candle—is memorable. All the same, weddings are easy.

But marriages are complex and difficult. In marriage we work out in every detail of life the promises and commitments spoken at the wedding. In marriage we develop the long and rich life of faithful love that the wedding announces. The event of the wedding without the life of marriage doesn't amount to much. It hardly matters if the man and woman dress up in their wedding clothes and re-enact the ceremony every anniversary and say "I'm married, I'm married, I'm married" if there is no daily love shared, if there is no continuing tenderness, no attentive listening, no inventive giving, no creative blessing.

Josiah's reform was like a wedding. Jeremiah's concern was with a marriage. It was a great achievement to repudiate Manasseh and establish the people in covenant with their God; but it was a lifelong career to embrace God's love and walk in his ways. The people celebrated Josiah's reform; they ignored Jeremiah's preaching. It is Jeremiah's lifelong achievement that the soggy religious mush of the masses never dulled his perceptions nor muted his insistent witness.

6 Go Down to the Potter's House

The word that came to Jeremiah from the LORD: "Arise, and go down to the potter's house, and there I will let you hear my words." So I went down to the potter's house, and there he was working at his wheel. And the vessel he was making of clay was spoiled in the potter's hand, and he reworked it into another vessel, as it seemed good to the potter to do.

Jeremiah 18:1-4

It is indeed by analogy that I believe the mind makes its richest movements, and it is by analogy that I believe the mind makes its deepest use of what it has understood; or at any rate I believe this to be an appropriate way of looking at the labor of the mind in a society, like ours, without a fixed character, and operating under a revelation which turns out to have been imperfectly understood. It is through analogy, if at all, that the falcon can again hear the falconer, that things can come together again, and that again the center can hold.

R. P. Blackmur[1]

W illi Ossa was an artist who worked as a janitor at night in a church on New York's West Side to support his wife and infant daughter. During the day he painted. German by birth, Willi grew up during the war years and then married an American girl, the daughter of an officer in the occupying army. I got to know Willi when I was a theological student working at the same church as an assistant pastor.

Willi liked to talk about religion; I liked to talk about art. We became friends. We got along well together and had long conversations. He decided to paint my portrait. I went to his house on West 92nd Street a couple of afternoons a week on my way to my work at the church and sat for thirty minutes or so for my portrait. He never permitted me to see what he was painting. Day after day, week after week, I sat while he painted. One day his wife came into the room and looked at the portrait now nearing completion and exclaimed in outrage, *"Krank, krank."* I knew just enough German to know that she was saying, "Sick! You paint him to look like a corpse!"

He answered, *"Nicht krank, aber keine Gnade"*—"he's not sick; that is the way he will look when the compassion is gone, when the mercy gets squeezed out of him."

A few half-understood phrases were enough for me to guess correctly, without seeing the portrait, what Willi was doing. We had often argued late into the night about the Christian faith. He hated the church. He thought Christians were hypocrites—all of them. He made a partial exception for me for friendship's sake. The Christians he had known had all collaborated with and blessed the Nazis. The Christians he had known were responsible for the death camps and the cremation of six million Jews. The Christians he had known had turned his beloved Germany into a pagan war machine. The word *Christian* was associated in Willi's experience with state church Christians who had been baptized and took communion and played Mozart all the while they led the nation into atrocities on a scale larger than anything the world had yet seen.

His argument was that the church squeezed the spirit and morality out of persons and reduced them to function in a bureaucracy where labels took the place of faces and rules took precedence over relationships. I would argue the other side. He would become vehement. Willi's English was adequate but not fluent; when he got excited he spoke German. "But there is no mercy in the church, *keine Gnade*, no compassion." He told me that I must never become a pastor. If I became a pastor, in twenty years I would be nothing but a hollow-eyed clerk good for nothing but desk work.

That was what he was painting day by day without my knowing it: a prophetic warning. A portrait not of what I was right then, but of what he was sure I would become if I persisted in the Christian way.

I have the portrait. I keep it in a closet and take it out to look at from time to time. The eyes are flat and empty. The face is gaunt and unhealthy. I was never convinced that what he painted was certain to happen—if I had been, I would not have become a pastor—but I knew it was possible. I knew that before I met Willi Ossa. I knew it from reading Scripture and from looking around me. But his artistic imagination created a portrait that was far more vivid than any verbal warning. The artist shows us what happens before it happens. The artist has eyes to connect the visible and the invisible and the skill to show us complete what we in our inattentive distraction see only in bits and pieces. So I look at that portrait, then look into the mirror and compare.

Master of Imagination

Jeremiah had an artistic imagination. It was one of the powerful imaginations in the history of our race. His imagination, used in the prophetic vocation, keeps us in touch with the reality of God and our essential lives. Jeremiah's imagination wakes us to the reality of God that permeates everything around us, shows us what our lives look like from the inside, and forces us to examine what we suppose we are doing and what God is doing in us.

Jeremiah, attentive and sensitive to God's direction, was commanded: "Arise, and go down to the potter's house, and there I will let you hear my words." God's task, through Jeremiah, is this: How can I get these people to take me seriously, right where they are? How can I get them to see that I am working, right now, silently and invisibly, but surely and eternally, in their lives and in their history? How can I get them to see the connections between what they are doing now and who they will be in ten years—in twenty years? How can I get them to see the continuities between what I did in Abraham and Moses and David and what they are now? How can I get them out of their tedious egos into my glorious will here and now? "Go down to the potter's house."

The great masters of the imagination do not make things up out of thin air; they direct our attention to what is right before our eyes. They then train us to see it whole—not in fragments but in context, with all the connections. They connect the visible and the invisible, the *this* with the *that*. They assist us in seeing what is around us all the time but which we regularly overlook. With their help we see it not as commonplace but as awesome, not as banal but as wondrous. For this reason the imagination is one of the essential ministries in nurturing the life of faith. For faith is not a leap out of the everyday but a plunge into its depths.

"Go down to the potter's house." Go down to the shoe-

maker's shop. Go down to the butcher's stall. Go down to
the grocer's stand. Go where the necessary, everyday work
is taking place. In our community he would have sent his
prophet to the gas station. In seventh-century Israel the
potter's house was a fixture in every community. The potter was a craftsman the location of whose house everyone
knew, whose activity was familiar to everyone, whose work
was necessary for the maintenance of everyday life.

"So I went down to the potter's house, and there he was
working at his wheel." Jeremiah watches the potter at work.
He is working at a wheel that has a formless mass of clay on
it. He turns the wheel and with skilled fingers shapes the
clay. A little pressure here, more there, a vessel begins to
rise out of that shapeless lump.

Do you realize how significant pottery is? The invention
of pottery set off a revolution. Before pottery there were
only wandering tribes, following herds of animals, going
from one food supply to another, forced here by drought,
there by famine. There was no time to develop anything,
no leisure to reflect on anything. It was hand-to-mouth
existence, day-to-day survival. But the invention of pottery
made it possible to store and carry. Then it was possible
to stay in a place for a while because grain could be stored
for next winter's meal and water carried. Then cooking
could be done and merchandise transported. The invention of pottery signaled a revolution and the revolution was
what we call civilization—the Neolithic Age.[2]

Try to imagine how life would change if we had no containers in which to store anything: no pots and pans, no
bowls and dishes, no buckets and jugs, no cans and bar-
rels, no cardboard boxes and brown paper bags, no grain
silos and no oil storage tanks. Life would be reduced to
what we could manage in a single day with what we could
hold in our hands at one time. Pottery made it possible
for communities to develop. Life was extended beyond

the immediate, beyond the urgent.

The practical impact of the invention of pottery is immense. But there is something else that is just as important. No one has ever been able to make a clay pot that is *just* a clay pot. Every pot is also an art form. Pottery is always changing its shape as potters find new proportions, different ways to shape the pots in pleasing combinations of curves. There is no pottery that besides being useful does not also show evidence of beauty. Pottery is artistically shaped, designed, painted, glazed, fired. It is one of the most functional items in life; it is also one of the most beautiful.

No one in Jeremiah's time ever put a piece of pottery on the mantel just to look at, using it to give a touch of elegance to a bare shelf. But neither, and this is just as significant, did anyone use a piece of pottery just because it was useful —always there was evidence of an artist's hand in it.

It is difficult for us to grasp the significance of that combination, for we live in a quite different world. We commonly separate the useful and the beautiful, the necessary and the elegant. We use brown paper bags for containers to which no one bothers to give shape or color or design. After all, we only want something in which to get our groceries home. Then we buy paintings to beautify the walls of our homes. We build featureless office buildings and ugly factories for our necessary work, then we build museums to contain the objects of beauty. But there have been times in history when these things were done better, when the necessary and the beautiful were integrated, when, in fact, it was impossible to think of separating them. For Jeremiah this was certainly the case: there were no brown paper bags and there were no museums, but there was pottery. Everywhere. Useful and beautiful. Functionally necessary and artistically elegant at one and the same time with no thought that the two elements could be separated.

Jeremiah's imagination went to work as he stood before

this potter with his lump of clay and his wheel. Jeremiah had seen potters at work all his life, but today he saw something else—he saw God at work making a people for his glory. A people of God. Persons created in the image of God. Necessary but not only necessary—each one also beautiful. And beautiful but not only beautiful—each one also necessary. Each human being is an inseparable union of necessity and freedom. There is no human being who is not useful with a part to play in what God is doing. And there is no human being who is not unique with special lines and colors and forms distinct from anyone else. All this came clear to Jeremiah in the potter's house: the brute fact of the clay, lumpish and inert, shaped for a purpose by the hands of the potter, and then, as it took shape, the realization of the uniquely designed individuality and wide-ranging usefulness it would acquire as a finished pot, painted and baked and glazed. God shapes us for his eternal purposes and he begins right here. The dust out of which we are made and the image of God into which we are made are one and the same.

The Pot Spoiled

And then the pot was spoiled: "the vessel he was making of clay was spoiled in the potter's hand."

Jeremiah knew all about that. He knew about spoiled vessels—men and women with impurities and blemishes that resist the shaping hand of the creator. He rubbed shoulders daily with people who were not useful: imperfections made their lives leak, holding neither wine nor water; a failure of proportion made their lives wobble or tip, unstable and undependable. Jeremiah had other words for it: sin, rebellion, self-will, wandering. But he had never had such a striking image for it.

Jeremiah continued to observe. What would the potter do now? Kick the wheel and go off in a sulk? Throw the

clay at the cat and go to the market and purchase another
brand? Neither. "He reworked it into another vessel, as it
seemed good to the potter to do." God kneads and presses,
pushes and pulls. The creative work starts over again, patiently, skillfully. God doesn't give up. God doesn't throw
away what is spoiled. Under a different image, George Herbert saw and said the same thing, "Storms are the triumph
of his art."[3]

Hope and Warning

Hope and warning join hands in this message: "Behold, like
the clay in the potter's hand, so are you in my hand, O house
of Israel" (Jer 18:6). He expands in both directions: "If that
nation, concerning which I have spoken, turns from its evil,
I will repent of the evil that I intended to do to it" (Jer 18:8).
On the other hand, "If it does evil in my sight, not listening
to my voice, then I will repent of the good which I had
intended to do to it" (Jer 18:10). No ominous prediction is
set in concrete dooming us. No rosy promise is license to
lazy indolence. "The clay can frustrate the potter's intention
and cause him to change it: as the quality of the clay determines what the potter can do with it, so the quality of a
people determines what God will do with them."[4]

The people refuse to respond, to participate, to willingly
involve themselves in the shaping purposes of God: "That
is in vain! We will follow our own plans, and will every one
act according to the stubbornness of his evil heart" (Jer
18:12). Do the people feel like they are stuck with their lives
and will simply make the best (or worst!) of what is there?
Jeremiah will not agree to their fatalism. He continues to
preach. He continues to confront. His visit to the potter's
house and his sermon about pottery-making are put to use
in making the people responsive to the God who is merci-
fully shaping their lives into what is useful and beautiful. In
such a setting even his judgments will be seen to be mercies.

In their recalcitrant, mulish unbelief the people will experience evil far beyond what they ever supposed possible, climaxing in the fall of Jerusalem and the Babylonian exile, but they will never be discarded.

God the Potter

This is one of Jeremiah's most powerful sermons. The image has captured the attention of people of faith everywhere. Not the least of the reasons for its effectiveness is that Jeremiah experienced it before he preached it. For no act of imagination, prophetic or artistic, is powerful if it is not wrought out of the inner life. This one had been working in Jeremiah's insides for a long time. The first word that Jeremiah heard from God was "Before I formed you in the womb I knew you" (Jer 1:5). The verb *formed* is *yatzar.* Now, as Jeremiah is prepared to set an image before the people by which they can understand themselves in relation to their God, he stands in the house of the *yotzer,* the potter. The word by which Jeremiah first learned to understand his own life, *yatzar,* is the word which is now used to let the people understand their lives: God shaped Jeremiah; God is shaping the people. God is a potter, a *yotzer,* working at his wheel on Jeremiah the lump of clay, on the people who are a lump of clay; he forms, *yatzar,* them. Jeremiah preaches to the people what he has lived himself.

All truth must be experienced personally before it is complete, before it is authentic. This truth, that God shapes us, that we are shaped by God, was Jeremiah's from the beginning. He had lived it in detail. He had been on that potter's wheel from before his birth. No word would mean more to Jeremiah than this one, *formed* by God. Jeremiah experienced his life as the created work of God. He was not a random accumulation of cells; he was formed by loving, skilled hands. He wasn't a potentiality of material just waiting for the lucky time when he could, by asserting his will, make something of his life; he was already made something by God, formed for his purposes.

The life of faith is very physical. Being a Christian is very much a matter of the flesh—of space and time and things. It means being thrown on the potter's wheel and shaped, our entire selves, into something useful and beautiful. And when we are not useful or beautiful we are reshaped. Painful, but worth it.

Willi Ossa's portrait shows me what I become if I drift from or deny a personal faith in a merciful God. Jeremiah's potter shows me what I become as I submit my life to the creative and merciful God. Our lives become the pottery that makes possible the emergence of civilization—what Jeremiah called the "people of God," what Jesus called the "kingdom of God," what Augustine called the "city of God." It is no longer every man for himself and the devil take the hindmost. We are containers, "regions of being" in Heiddeger's words, in which love and salvation and mercy are conserved and shared. Everything is connected and makes sense now—the shape of creation and the shape of salvation, God's shaping hand and the shape of my life.

7 Pashhur Beat Jeremiah

Now Pashhur the priest, the son of Immer, who was chief officer in the house of the LORD, heard Jeremiah prophesying these things. Then Pashhur beat Jeremiah the prophet, and put him in the stocks that were in the upper Benjamin Gate of the house of the LORD. On the morrow, when Pashhur released Jeremiah from the stocks, Jeremiah said to him, "The LORD does not call your name Pashhur, but Terror on every side."

Jeremiah 20:1-3

Contrary to what might be expected, I look back on experiences that at the time seemed especially desolating and painful with particular satisfaction. Indeed, I can say with complete truthfulness that everything I have learned in my seventy-five years in this world, everything that has truly enhanced and enlightened my existence, has been through affliction and not through happiness, whether pursued or attained. In other words, if it ever were to be possible to eliminate affliction from our earthly existence by means of some drug or other medical mumbo jumbo . . . the result would not be to make life delectable, but to make it too banal and trivial to be endurable. This, of course, is what the Cross signifies. And it is the Cross, more than anything else, that has called me inexorably to Christ."

Malcolm Muggeridge[1]

My first assignment after being ordained as a pastor almost finished me. I was called to be the assistant pastor in a large and affluent suburban church. I was glad to be part of such an obviously winning organization. After I had been there a short time, a few people came to me and asked that I lead them in a Bible study. "Of course," I said, "there is nothing I would rather do." We met on Monday evenings. There weren't many—eight or nine men and women —but even so that was triple the two or three that Jesus defined as a quorum. They were eager and attentive; I was full of enthusiasm. After a few weeks the senior pastor, my boss, asked me what I was doing on Monday evenings. I told him. He asked me how many people were there. I told him. He told me that I would have to stop.

"Why?" I asked.

"It is not cost-effective. That is too few people to spend your time on."

I was told then how I should spend my time. I was introduced to the principles of successful church administration: crowds are important, individuals are expendable; the positive must always be accented, the negative must be suppressed. Don't expect too much of people—your job is to make them feel good about themselves and about the church. Don't talk too much about abstractions like God and sin—deal with practical issues. We had an elaborate music program, expensively and brilliantly executed. The sermons were seven minutes long and of the sort that Father Taylor (the sailor-preacher in Boston who was the model for Father Mapple in Melville's *Moby Dick*) complained of in the transcendentalists of the last century: that a person could no more be converted listening to sermons like that than get intoxicated drinking skim milk.[2]

It was soon apparent that I didn't fit. I had supposed that I was there to be a pastor: to proclaim and interpret Scripture, to guide people into a life of prayer, to encourage faith, to represent the mercy and forgiveness of Christ at special times of need, to train people to live as disciples in their families, in their communities and in their work. In fact I had been hired to help run a church and do it as efficiently as possible: to be a cheerleader to this dynamic organization, to recruit members, to lend the dignity of my office to certain ceremonial occasions, to promote the image of a prestigious religious institution.

I got out of there as quickly as I could decently manage it. At the time I thought I had just been unlucky. Later I came to realize that what I experienced was not at all uncommon. Those contrasting expectations and the conflicts that grow out of them are a major theme in the history of religion.

Conflicting Expectations
Some people come to church looking for a way to make life better, to feel good about themselves, to see things in a better light. They arrange a ritual and hire a preacher to make that happen for them. Other people come to church because they want God to save and rule them. They accept the fact that there are temptations and sufferings and sacrifices involved in leaving a way of life in which they are in control and plunging into an uncertain existence in which God is in control. One group of people sees religion as a way to successful happy living; nothing that interferes with the success or interrupts the happiness will be tolerated. The other group sees religion as a way in which hurt, flawed and damaged persons become whole in relation to God; anything will be accepted (mockery, pain, renunciation, self-denial) in order to deepen and extend that reality.

One way is the way of enhancing what I want; the other

way is a commitment of myself to become what God wants. Always and everywhere these contrasting expectations are in evidence. They are conspicuous in the experience of Jeremiah and collide in a noisy and dramatic confrontation one day in Jerusalem.

The Popular Preacher

In Jeremiah's lifetime there was a terrific revival of religion. The reform that King Josiah launched cleaned up the country and made the truth of God known and the worship of God popular. Jeremiah was one of the preachers of the reform. He was, no doubt, delighted that people were thronging the temple. He could hardly fail to be pleased that Scripture was once again known and preached.

The most popular preacher in Jerusalem during those years, though, was probably Pashhur. Pashhur was the chief overseer in the temple in Jerusalem, a man of prominence. When you saw him at the head of the flourishing religious establishment, the temple, you could not help feeling better. His enthusiasm was electric. When he stretched out his arms in blessing, everyone, from the least to the greatest, knew that they were included. Everyone loved to hear him: he was positive, affirmative, confident. He had the ability to draw out the best from everything. He was able to search the Scriptures and find texts that made the darkest days bright.

Living is difficult. There is much that goes wrong. We lay our plans carefully and things still go badly. We try to get ahead, but unaccountably something interferes, and we end up flat on our faces. Accidents. Weather. The general cussedness of life. Murphy's Law. In the midst of this there are some men and women who make it all seem better. There is a tone in their voices that dispels gloom. They have a smile that is infectious. They say that everything is going to be all right, and we believe them.

It is no small advantage to have a place to go from time to time for this kind of pick-up, to have a person who will perform this function for us—a place like the temple, a person like Pashhur. He saw the positive dimension in everything. He interpreted the current scene in such a way that anxieties were allayed and fears banished. Pashhur was a national asset. He had a host of imitators, prophets and priests and teachers who specialized in finding ways to massage the national psyche. Flannery O'Connor described one of their twentieth-century descendants: "He is really a combination minister and masseur."[3] Their favorite word was peace: "Everything is going to be all right; God is working out his purposes in us; we are God's people; and he will bless all the people of the earth through us." They celebrated the illustrious past—Moses the liberator, Joshua the conqueror, David the sweet psalmist of Israel, Solomon splendid in wisdom and riches. With such blood flowing in their veins the people knew they were members of an inviolable elect.

There were, to be sure, a few problems: an inordinate amount of crime, scandalous reports of injustice, a widening gap between the rich and the poor. And even though the religious life of the people had been cleaned up in public, it was an open secret that all the old fertility rites were being practiced in out-of-the-way places in the country ("beside every green tree, and on the high hills, on the mountains in the open country"—Jer 17:2-3). What the reform movement had managed mostly was to get the scandalous behavior out of sight and make church-going popular again.

But that did not daunt the positive thinking of Pashhur. The people loved him. They crowded the temple to be reassured by his sonorous baritone, to be cheered by his dazzling smile: "God loves you. . . . Peace, peace, peace."

Peace, Peace, but No Peace

There was one man in Jerusalem who was not impressed by Pashhur. Jeremiah couldn't stomach him. In angry exasperation Jeremiah cried out, "From prophet to priest every one deals falsely. They have healed the wound of my people lightly, saying, 'Peace, peace,' when there is no peace" (Jer 8:10-11).

The task of a prophet is not to smooth things over but to make things right. The function of religion is not to make people feel good but to make them good. Love? Yes, God loves us. But his love is passionate and seeks faithful, committed love in return. God does not want tame pets to fondle and feed; he wants mature, free people who will respond to him in authentic individuality. For that to happen there must be honesty and truth. The self must be toppled from its pedestal. There must be pure hearts and clear intelligence, confession of sin and commitment in faith.

And peace? Yes, God gives peace. But it is not a peace that gets along with everyone by avoiding the hint of anything unpleasant. It is not a peace achieved by refusing to talk about painful subjects or touch sore spots. It is a peace that is hard won by learning to pray. There is evil to combat, apathy to defeat, dullness to challenge, ambition to confront. There are persons all around us, children and parents, youth and adults, who are being trampled and violated, who are being hurt and despised. Any preaching of peace that turns its back on these is a cruel farce.

There is nothing wrong with success, and there is nothing wrong with applause. It is not evidence of a sellout when a preacher has a crowd of people before him, and it is not proof of superficiality when a church is full. Nor, to take the other side, is it a sign of integrity that a man is persecuted and run out of town for what he says. He may, in fact, be a dangerous fraud. Nor can poverty be claimed as proof of courageous authenticity—the person may be

simply incompetent. What is wrong is to evaluate the worth
of words and deeds by their popularity. What is scandalous
is to approve only what is applauded. What is disastrous is
to assume that only the celebrated is genuine.

There are times when the truth will receive a wide hearing and times when it will not. Jesus had a congregation of
five thousand one day and four women and two bored sol-
diers another. His message was the same both days. We
must learn to live by the truth, not by our feelings, not by
the world's opinion, not by what the latest statistical survey
tells us is the accepted morality, not by what the advertisers
tell us is the most gratifying lifestyle. We are trained in the
biblical faith to take lightly what the experts say, the scholars say, the pollsters say, the politicians say, the pastors say.
We are trained to listen to the Word of God, to test everything against what God reveals to us in Christ, to discover
all meaning and worth by examining life in relation to
God's will.

Despotic Egos

Jeremiah's task was to challenge the lies and speak the
truth. Why do we so easily swallow the lies? Why do we find
it so difficult to accept the truth? Because we are looking
for bargains. We want shortcuts. There are no easy ways.
There is only one way. If we are going to be complete human beings, we are going to have to do it with God. We will
have to be rescued from these despotic egos that reduce us
to something less than human. We will have to expose the
life of self-centeredness and proclaim the truth of God-
centeredness.

Jeremiah wanted his people to practice adoration of God
—something full-blooded and soaring—instead of mincing
around the temple preening themselves before the mirrors
of self-admiration. He arranged for a conference with
some of the leaders of the city. He took them three or four

hundred yards south of the temple to the Valley of Hinnom at the site of Topheth. Child sacrifice had been carried out there and still was being done in secret. It was the garbage dump of the city. The place stank.

Jeremiah had a pottery water jug under his arm. He spoke his concern to the leaders. He told them that God had immense love and holy purposes for them. He said what he had said so many times, that a reform is useless if it does not change people's lives. It is no good polishing up the brass in the temple if the quality of people's lives is left unattended in their poverty. It is no good obeying the letter of the commands written in Deuteronomy if the spirit of love that permeates Deuteronomy is ignored. It is no good being enthusiastic over the great religious traditions if the people we don't like are treated like scum. It is no good adoring religious ceremony and ritual that make us feel good if the feelings never get connected with good actions. Truth is inward: we must experience within ourselves that which we profess. Truth is social: we must share with others what we profess. Statistics are a farce. Popularity is a smoke screen. All that matters is God.

Standing with these leaders in this place of dreadful reminders, Jeremiah accused them of going along with a religion that assured them of success in whatever they undertook at the same time that they were abandoning the God who called them to live in love and faith. He accused them of taking their religion from the world around them, making a religious ritual out of the gratification of lust, handing out religious formulas for financial prosperity. When he finished his short speech, Jeremiah broke the pottery decanter by throwing it to the ground: "Thus says the LORD of hosts: So will I break this people and this city, as one breaks a potter's vessel, so that it can never be mended" (Jer 19:11).

Terror on Every Side

Word traveled fast. By the time Jeremiah got back to the temple area the city was buzzing. Pashhur, of course, heard. Pashhur as chief overseer of the temple was responsible for maintaining the successful operation. A man like Jeremiah was no help. Pashhur arrested him and put him in the stocks on the north side of the temple area. Jeremiah was humiliated, but not intimidated. He spoke as sharply as ever to Pashhur. Putting Jeremiah in the stocks confined him, but it did not silence him. He yelled at Pashhur, "The LORD does not call your name Pashhur but *Magor-missabib*, Terror-on-every-side. Judgment is coming because of willful, selfish, entrenched sin, and all you do is sprinkle holy water on it. Babylon will invade this place and plunder everything and take the people captive. When that happens Pashhur, your name will be remembered as *Magor-missabib*, Terror-on-every-side. It will be obvious then that you, not me, are responsible for disturbing the peace. The falseness of your preaching will be exposed, the hypocrisy of your success cult will be on display and because of it inescapable judgment. *Magor-missabib* indeed, Terror-on-every side."

This wasn't the first time that Jeremiah had used that phrase. He had spoken it frequently enough so that it was associated with him. We have references to it in three other sermons (Jer 6:25; 46:5; 49:29). Putting the tag on Pashhur was, under the circumstances, futile. Pashhur was the honored chief officer of the temple, presiding over splendid rituals and applauded by crowds of people; Jeremiah was in the stocks—a laughingstock. That day, as people went to the temple and passed Jeremiah, someone picked up the phrase that he had used so often and turned it against him as a mocking nickname. Soon the crowd was chanting in derision of Jeremiah, "There's old *Magor-missabib*, Terror-on-every-side."[4]

Jeremiah's humiliation was complete: an object of ridicule in the stocks, taunted with the name *Magor-missabib.* The word that had been forged out of suffering and articulated out of concern for the perilous existence of his people was now a slogan of contempt: *Magor-missabib,* Terror-on-every-side; *Magor-missabib,* old fire-and-brimstone himself!

Bronze Walls
Unafraid of the stocks. Unintimidated by the taunts. Undeterred by humiliation, or embarrassment, or insecurity, or pain, or failure, or doubt. "A fortified city, an iron pillar, and bronze walls" indeed!

We don't have to like it. Jeremiah didn't like it. He yelled at Pashhur, and after he yelled at Pashhur he yelled at God, angry, hurt and somewhat bewildered that all this was happening to him (Jer 20:7-10). He didn't like any of it, but he wasn't afraid of it because the most important thing in his life was God—not comfort, not applause, not security, but the living God. What he did fear was worship without astonishment, religion without commitment. He feared getting what he wanted and missing what God wanted. It is still the only thing worthy of our fear.

What a waste it would be to take these short, precious, eternity-charged years that we are given and squander them in cocktail chatter when we can be, like Jeremiah, vehemently human and passionate with God.

8 My Wound Incurable

O LORD, thou knowest;
  remember me and visit me, . . .
I did not sit in the company of merrymakers,
  nor did I rejoice;
I sat alone, because thy hand was upon me,
  for thou hadst filled me with indignation.
Why is my pain unceasing,
  my wound incurable,
  refusing to be healed?
Wilt thou be to me like a deceitful brook,
  like waters that fail?

Jeremiah 15:15, 17-18

Talking to God, I felt, is always better than talking about God; those pious conversations—there's always a touch of self-approval about them.

Therese of Lisieux[1]

Indisputably great persons arouse curiosity. What are they like on the inside? What do they do when they are not being watched? What goes on in their private lives? Our appetite for gossip, for confessions, for inside information is insatiable. For every person who reads the front page story on a politician's speech there are twenty who will read the gossip column that describes in delicious detail his companion at dinner the night before. We want, we say, to know what a person is *really* like. We are not content with the public image, the outer event, the external happening. We pounce on any detail, however insignificant, that might reveal what goes on behind the scenes in the heart.

Often this curiosity is a sniping pettiness that wants to cut people down to our size so that we will not be embarrassed in our own littleness. It is the kind of sleazy attitude that Harry Stack Sullivan found so disreputable: "If I have to be a mole hill, by God there are going to be no mountains." But there is an avid interest in the personal details of a great person's life that is healthy. It is the instinctive search for the essentially human that establishes a link of kinship with the rest of us.

What was Jeremiah really like? What did he do when he was alone? When no one was watching, how did he conduct himself? Where there was no audience to address, how did he behave? What did Jeremiah do when he was not staging confrontations with the religious leaders of Jerusalem? What did he do when he was not standing the people on their ears with his thundering prophecies? What did he do when he wasn't colliding with temple officials and upsetting the status quo? What did he do when he was not making headlines?

A Praying Prophet

There is a single, clear, straightforward answer to these questions: he prayed. Seven passages in the book of Jeremiah are labeled "confessional."[2] In each of these Jeremiah speaks in the first person. He opens his heart. He reveals what is going on inside while the fireworks are going off outside. We hold our breath on the brink of these most private revelations. We have been so often disappointed, even disillusioned, when we have gained access to the diaries, letters, tapes of great and admired people. How many public reputations can survive a thorough exposure of the inner life?[3]

Jeremiah's inner life is revealed in these confessions. We are surprised, but we are not disillusioned. When Jeremiah was out of the public eye he was passionate with God—he prayed. Jeremiah's secret life is a prayer life. The cellar reality of Jeremiah's towering humanity is prayer.

A look at Jeremiah in secret does not show him with a few cronies in a bull session swapping stories about God, catching up on the rumors of God. God is not someone or something to be talked *about.* Nor do we find Jeremiah in a library studying up on God. He did not pore over the volumes from Babylonia in order to analyze their beliefs. He did not examine the burial practices of the Egyptians to discover what might be learned about their concept of immortality. God is not an idea to be studied. And we don't find Jeremiah at his desk with pen and paper using his sharp mind and comprehensive intelligence to work out answers to the question of God ("How can it be that a good God permits an evil time?"). God is not a problem to be solved.

What we find is Jeremiah *praying:* addressing God, listening to God. Prayer is the act in which we approach God as living person, a *thou* to whom we speak, not an *it* that we talk about. Prayer is the attention that we give to the one who attends to us. It is the decision to approach God as the personal center, as our Lord and our Savior, our entire lives gathered up and expressed in the approach. Prayer is personal language raised to the highest degree. These seven confessional passages show Jeremiah in his unguarded and most personal times saying *I* and *Thou*.

The Intimacy of Prayer

Nearly everyone believes in God and throws casual offhand remarks in his general direction from time to time. But prayer is something quite different. Suppose yourself at dinner with a person whom you very much want to be with —a friend, a lover, a person important to you. The dinner is in a fine restaurant where everything is arranged to give you a sense of privacy. There is adequate illumination at your table with everything else in shadow. You are aware of other persons and other activity in the room, but they do not intrude on your intimacy. There is talking and listening. There are moments of silence, full of meaning. From time to time a waiter comes to your table. You ask questions of him; you place your order with him; you ask to have your glass refilled; you send the broccoli back because it arrived cold; you thank him for his attentive service and leave a tip. You depart, still in companionship with the person with whom you dined, but out on the street conversation is less personal, more casual.

That is a picture of prayer. The person with whom we set aside time for intimacy, for this deepest and most personal conversation, is God. At such times the world is not banished, but it is in the shadows, on the periphery. Prayer is never complete and unrelieved solitude; it is, though, carefully protected and skillfully supported intimacy. Prayer is the desire to listen to God firsthand, to speak to God firsthand, and then setting aside the time and making the arrangements to do it. It issues from the conviction that the living God is immensely important to me and that what goes on between us demands my exclusive attention.

But there is a parody of prayer that we engage in all too often. The details are the same but with two differences: the person across the table is Self and the waiter is God. This waiter-God is essential but peripheral. You can't have the dinner without him, but he is not an intimate participant in it. He is someone to whom you give orders, make complaints, and maybe, at the end, give thanks. The person you are absorbed in is Self—your moods, your ideas, your interests, your satisfactions or lack of them. When you leave the restaurant you forget about the waiter until the next time. If it is a place to which you go regularly, you might even remember his name.

The confessions of Jeremiah are no parody but the real thing—exclusive focus on God: intense, undivided preoccupation with God. This accounts for much that is powerful and attractive in Jeremiah. Here is the source of the personal intensity and incorruptible integrity that is so impressive in Jeremiah.

What goes on in these intimate exchanges between Jeremiah and God? We know who he is *with* in secret; what does he *say* in secret? The confession in Jeremiah 15 is a fair sample. Here some of us are in for another surprise, for the uninstructed idea of prayer is that it is accepting and soothing, that the person at prayer is the person at peace in the universe. But Jeremiah at prayer is scared, lonely, hurt and angry.

> *O LORD, thou knowest;*
> *remember me and visit me,*
> *and take vengeance for me on my persecutors.*

Jeremiah was frightened. Cursed and hunted down, there was no secure place for him. The plots against his life and the physical beatings and cruel confinements that he suffered all come out in this prayer. He is speaking to God

what he is experiencing. It is clear that he neither accepted
it or liked it: "God, you got me into this, now get me out!"

He continues by contrasting his own sense of urgency
with God's deliberate patience.

> *In thy forbearance take me not away;*
> *know that for thy sake I bear reproach. (Jer 15:15)*

John Bright translates with more clarity: "Do not through
thy patience destroy me! Consider! For thy sake I suffer
abuse." Which seems to mean, "Don't be so lenient with my
persecutors that they have time to destroy me."[4] There is
desperation in that sentence. Jeremiah struggles to accommodate his awareness of God's unhurried, measured pace
with the panicky fear that time is running out on him. The
mills of God turn slowly while the engines of persecution
run exceedingly swift. Our compulsive timetables collide
with God's leisurely providence. We tell God not only what
to do but when to do it. We take him seriously—why else
would we be praying?—but we take ourselves more seriously, telling him exactly what he must do for us and when.

Loneliness

Jeremiah next prays his loneliness.

> *Thy words were found, and I ate them,*
> *and thy words became to me a joy*
> *and the delight of my heart;*
> *for I am called by thy name,*
> *O LORD, God of hosts.*
> *I did not sit in the company of merrymakers,*
> *nor did I rejoice;*
> *I sat alone, because thy hand was upon me,*
> *for thou hadst filled me with indignation. (Jer 15:16-17)*

From the first Jeremiah received God's word with enthusiasm. There may be a reference here to the discovery of the
Deuteronomy scroll in the temple which Jeremiah wel-
comed and then threw himself into the task of preaching

as spokesman for the reform commanded by Josiah. It was delightful work but a lonely business. It meant years of solitude. The laughing, merrymaking majority went its way, and Jeremiah went his in lonely reflection, finding the meaning of God's word and preaching its lived truth. Jeremiah was constitutionally unable to say something just because he was told it was true: he *lived* the truth and then he spoke it. There was delight in living that way. He gave himself without reserve to this way of life that meant taking God's word more seriously than any human word. But having plunged into this way, he found that no one was with him. He was all by himself. What would he do? Go back to the party until others decided to come along? He couldn't do that. He was committed. Having acquired a taste for God's truth, he could not return to the bland diet of gossip and rumor. All the same it was a lonely business.

Hurt

He goes on to pray his hurt.

Why is my pain unceasing,
    my wound incurable,
    refusing to be healed?

The sin of the people, the cruelty of the wicked, the giddy indifference of the everyday crowd—all this was a deep wound in Jeremiah. He hurt because he cared. He had undertaken to speak for God, to speak that eternal love to this fickle people. Now he felt in his own being all the aching hurt of unrequited love. Having identified so thoroughly with God's message, he also felt the rejection in every bone and muscle. Their blasphemies cut him; their clumsy rebellions bruised him; their thoughtless rituals salted his open wounds. And there was no cure in sight, for the only cure was a people who repent and trust God. He looked in vain for any intimation of that.

Anger

The prayer intensifies. Turning from his hurt, now, in an audacious burst, he prays his anger.

Wilt thou be to me like a deceitful brook,
like waters that fail?

He calls God to task. Once he had preached that God was "the fountain of living waters" (Jer 2:13); now he accuses him of being a "deceitful brook"—one of those stream beds in the desert that looks as if water should be flowing in it but when you arrive at its banks it is dry. Water only flows in it after a rain; it cannot be depended upon between times. What he says in effect is "God, you have tricked me. You promised but you did not deliver."

Jeremiah was not timid in his prayers. An even bolder accusation came later when he raged, "You seduced me, Yahweh, and I let you; You seized and overcame me" (Jer 20:7 Bright's translation). A blunt but literal rendering is "First you seduced me, then you raped me." You lured me by enticing words, then you seized me by force and made me submit to your will.[5] Our anger can be a measure of our faith. Believers argue with God; skeptics argue with each other.

That is Jeremiah at prayer: scared, lonely, hurt, angry. A surprise? The indomitable Jeremiah praying like that? All of us experience these things. No one alive is a stranger to them. But do we pray them? Jeremiah prayed them. Everything he experienced and thought he set in relationship to a living, knowing, saving God. And the moment these things are set in relationship to God something begins to happen.

Repentance

Jeremiah stops speaking but the prayer continues, for prayer does not end when we end. In prayer God is not merely audience, he is partner. Jeremiah has spoken honestly, now he listens expectantly.

> *Therefore thus says the LORD:*
> *"If you return, I will restore you,*
>   *and you shall stand before me." (Jer 15:19)*

Return/repent. This is one of the key words in Jeremiah's preaching. Now the message that he has been delivering to the people is delivered to him. Could it be that his pouring out of pain is tinged with self-pity? God responds: "The fright, the loneliness, the hurt, the anger—I understand that, Jeremiah, but I won't indulge you in it. Don't wallow in it. Turn away from it. Repent. If you turn (from such talk) then I will turn you (restore you) to the prophetic office." Throughout this passage there is a play on the word *return/repent.* [6]

Jeremiah's part in the prayer was to be honest and personal; it is *God* with whom he has to do. The first requirement in a personal relationship is to be ourselves. Off with the masks. Away with the pretense. "It's *me,* it's *me,* it's *me,* O Lord." Jeremiah's prayer is not pious, not nice, not proper—he speaks what he feels, and he feels scared, lonely, hurt and angry. Well enough. *God's part* in the prayer is to restore and save. Before God in prayer we do not remain the same. The fright and loneliness and pain and accusation are all there, but they do not stay there. Part (not all) of what Jeremiah was doing was feeling sorry for himself on his knees. God feels our pains, but he does not indulge our self-pity. God is severe with Jeremiah as Jeremiah was severe with the people: "Repent. Turn away from that kind of feeling for it is destructive. Then I will restore you, and you will stand upright, ready to serve again, in my presence."

Re-establishing Priorities
God's response continues.

> *If you utter what is precious, and not what is worthless,*

you shall be as my mouth.
They shall turn to you,
  but you shall not turn to them.

Jeremiah was discouraged, understandably, because his words accomplished nothing. His preaching was futile. All he got for his pains was persecution and reproach. Should he change his tune and speak the trash the people loved to hear? God stiffens his resolve. Stick to your calling; you shall be as my mouth. "Let *them* come over to you; don't *you* go over to them" (Bright's translation). Jeremiah was concerned about what people were saying; that is not his concern. *God* is his concern.

Priorities are re-established in prayer. It makes all the difference in the world whether God is in the first place or in the second. Who is in the first place here? God or the people? If it is God who is in first place, the complaints express only what is involved in a tough job. The job is either worth doing or it is not. What do I really want to do with my life, love others or flatter them, please others or please God?

The setting of priorities is not a once-for-all act. It has to be redone frequently. Balances shift. Circumstances change. Moods swing. Is it still God, in fact, with whom I have first of all to do, or is it not? Prayer is the place where the priorities are re-established.

Renewal

Jeremiah continues to listen. He hears this.

And I will make you to this people
  a fortified wall of bronze;
they will fight against you,
  but they shall not prevail over you,
for I am with you
  to save you and deliver you, says the LORD.
I will deliver you out of the hand of the wicked,
  and redeem you from the grasp of the ruthless.

He had heard these words once, in his youth (Jer 1:18-19). Everything God said then he says still. The promise is still in effect.

It is not enough to remember; we must *hear* it again. Prayer is the act in which we hear it again. It is not enough to carry memory verses around with us; we need daily encounter with the resonant voice of God. Prayer is that encounter. Situations change. Does God change? We pray. We listen. God speaks his word again—the same word!—and we are restored and renewed in our commitment.

Three words, somewhat synonymous, conclude: *save you . . . deliver you . . . redeem you.* "The total picture of deliverance is many-sided and each verb provides a different emphasis."[7] The live connection between God's call and Jeremiah's commitment is reaffirmed. The personal relationship, the covenant connection, has been subject to a thousand stresses and called into question a hundred times. What Walter Lippmann called the "acids of modernity" eat away at the sinews and thongs that connect our lives with God's purposes.[8] Life is moving and dynamic, changing and growing. The world challenges and attacks. The word of God does not change and my call does not change, but the relationship is under constant assault and must be renewed constantly. Resolve is essential but not enough. In prayer God provides renewal. Prayer is not so much the place where we learn something new, but where God confirms anew the faith to which we are committed.

Running the Race
The marathon is one of the most strenuous athletic events in sport. The Boston Marathon attracts the best runners in the world. The winner is automatically placed among the great athletes of our time. In the spring of 1980, Rosie Ruiz was the first woman to cross the finish line. She had the laurel wreath placed on her head in a blaze of lights and cheering.

She was completely unknown in the world of running.
An incredible feat! Her first race a victory in the prestigious
Boston Marathon! Then someone noticed her legs—loose
flesh, cellulite. Questions were asked. No one had seen
her along the 26.2 mile course. The truth came out: she
had jumped into the race during the last mile.

There was immediate and widespread interest in Rosie.
Why would she do that when it was certain that she would
be found out? Athletic performance cannot be faked. But
she never admitted her fraud. She repeatedly said that she
would run another marathon to validate her ability. Somehow she never did. People interviewed her, searching for
a clue to her personality. One interviewer concluded that
she really believed that she had run the complete Boston
Marathon and won. She was analyzed as a sociopath. She
lied convincingly and naturally with no sense of conscience,
no sense of reality in terms of right and wrong, acceptable
and unacceptable behavior. She appeared bright, normal
and intelligent. But there was no moral sense to give co-
herence to her social actions.

In reading about Rosie I thought of all the people I know
who want to get in on the finish but who cleverly arrange
not to run the race. They appear in church on Sunday
wreathed in smiles, entering into the celebration, but there
is no personal life that leads up to it or out from it. Occa-
sionally they engage in spectacular acts of love and compassion in public. We are impressed, but surprised, for they
were never known to do that before. Yet, you never know.
Better give them the benefit of the doubt. Then it turns
out to be a stunt: no personal involvement either precedes
or follows the act. They are plausible and convincing. But
in the end they do not run the race, believing through the
tough times, praying through the lonely, angry, hurt hours.
They have no sense for what is *real* in religion. The proper
label for such a person is *religiopath*.

No one becomes human the way Jeremiah was human by posing in a posture of victory. It was his prayers, hidden but persistent, that brought him to the human wholeness and spiritual sensitivity that we want. What we do in secret determines the soundness of who we are in public. Prayer is the secret work that develops a life that is thoroughly authentic and deeply human.

9 Twenty-Three Years... Persistently

*For twenty-three years, from the thirteenth year of Josiah
the son of Amon, king of Judah, to this day, the word of the
LORD has come to me, and I have spoken persistently to you, but
you have not listened. You have neither listened nor inclined
your ears to hear, although the LORD persistently sent to
you all his servants the prophets, saying, "Turn now, every one
of you, from his evil way and wrong doings, and dwell upon
the land which the LORD has given to you and your fathers
from of old and for ever."*

Jeremiah 25:3-5

Experienced mountaineers have a quiet, regular, short
step—on the level it looks petty; but then this step they
keep up, on and on as they ascend, whilst the inexperienced townsman hurries along, and soon has to
stop, dead beat with the climb.... Such an expert
mountaineer, when the thick mists come, halts and
camps out under some slight cover brought with him,
quietly smoking his pipe, and moving on only when the
mist has cleared away.... You want to grow in virtue,
to serve God, to love Christ? Well, you will grow
in and attain to these things if you will make them a
slow and sure, an utterly real, a mountain stepplod
and ascent, willing to have to camp for weeks or months
in spiritual desolation, darkness and emptiness at

different stages in your march and growth. All demand for constant light, for ever the best—the best to your own feeling, all attempt at eliminating or minimizing the cross and trial, is so much soft folly and puerile trifling.

Baron Friedrich von Hügel[1]

The difference between the right word and the almost right word is, said Mark Twain, the difference between lightning and a lightning bug. A single word, if it is the right word, can illuminate and strike fire all at once. In Jeremiah 25 at the center of the book of Jeremiah and spoken at the midpoint of his prophetic career, there is one of these right words: persistently, *hashkem*.

The word has a picture behind it. *Shechem* means shoulder. At the center of Palestine there are two immense shoulder mountains, Ebal and Gerazim. The village nestled between these massive shoulders is named Shechem. When the Israelites first came into the land after their forty years of wandering in the wilderness, Joshua led them to Shechem, lined them up on the slopes of the two shoulder mountains, half on one slope and half on the other, and reviewed the word of God that had directed them there. From one shoulder the blessings that would come from a life of worshipful trust were called out; from the other shoulder the curses that would come from a life of rebellious self-centeredness were called out. Shechem—the center where the word of God was spoken and listened to.

Then, as words do, *shechem* developed another meaning. When you went on a trip in those days you loaded provisions for the journey on your donkey's shoulders, or put them on your own shoulders, and set out. So the noun, shoulder, developed into a verb that meant "load the shoulders of beasts for a day's journey."[2] In a hot country like Israel it was important to get in as many miles as possible before the sun came up and fatigued you, so such journeys characteristically began long before dawn. Eventually the word came to describe the activity of people who got up early before the sun and set out with heavy burdens on long journeys.[3] They got up early in order to have as many hours as possible to do what they intended to do.

This is the form of the word that is used here at the center of Jeremiah—the unwobbling pivot of his life and his book. "For twenty-three years . . . the word of the LORD has come to me, and I have spoken persistently [*hashkem*] to you, but you have not listened." For twenty-three years Jeremiah got up every morning and listened to God's word. For twenty-three years Jeremiah got up every morning and spoke God's word to the people. For twenty-three years the people slept in, sluggish and indolent, and heard nothing.

The word is not only at the center of Jeremiah's book and his life, it is spread out across his ministry. There are eleven instances:

7:13   *And now, because you have done all these things, says the LORD, and when I spoke to you* persistently *you did not listen, and when I called you, you did not answer . . .*

7:25-26 *From the day that your fathers came out of the land of Egypt to this day, I have* persistently *sent all my servants the prophets to them, day after day; yet they did not listen to me . . .*

11:7-8   *For I solemnly warned your fathers when I brought them up out of the land of Egypt, warning them* persistently, *even to this day, saying, Obey my voice. Yet they did not obey or incline their ear . . .*

25:3   *For twenty-three years, from the thirteenth year of Josiah the son of Amon, king of Judah, to this day, the word of the LORD has come to me, and I have spoken* persistently *to you, but you have not listened.*

25:4   *You have neither listened nor inclined your ears to hear, although the LORD* persistently *sent to you all his servants the prophets . . .*

26:5   *. . . to heed the words of my servants the prophets whom I send to you* urgently, *though you have not heeded . . .*

29:19   *. . . because they did not heed my words, says the LORD,*

>   *which I* persistently *sent to you by my servants the*
>   *prophets, but you would not listen, says the LORD.*
>
> 32:33   *They have turned to me their back and not their face;*
>   *and though I have taught them* persistently *they have*
>   *not listened to receive instruction.*
>
> 35:14   *I have spoken to you* persistently, *but you have not*
>   *listened to me.*
>
> 35:15   *I have sent to you all my servants the prophets, sending*
>   *them* persistently, *saying, "Turn now every one of you*
>   *from his evil way, and amend your doings . . .*
>
> 44:4   *Yet I* persistently *sent to you all my servants the proph-*
>   *ets, saying, "Oh, do not do this abominable thing that*
>   *I hate!"*

Does that sound like a grim business? Tough sledding?
There is no question but that it was difficult. We know that
Jeremiah suffered an enormous amount of abuse across
those years. He faced mockery and rejection and imprison-
ment. He wrestled with stretches of discouragement and
pits of despair and thought of quitting. What difference
did it make anyway? Why not adjust to the mediocrities
of the age?

At one of those times God confronted Jeremiah: "If
you're tired from running a footrace, how will you race
against horses?" (Jer 12:5 Bright's translation). What do
you want, Jeremiah, a tame, domesticated life? A Sunday
stroll with these bloated and cretinous people who are living like parasites? Or will you compete against horses? The
confrontation galvanized Jeremiah out of his enervating
despair: "I want to run with the horses." The next morning
he was again up before dawn, living *persistently* and *urgently*.

A Ready Heart

The word *hashkem* ("persistently") has a sunrise in it. Jeremiah is up before the sun to do his work. He is no reluctant,
bored drudge. There is an early morning lightness in him.

Every day there is the anticipation of listening to God's word and then speaking God's word. Jeremiah almost certainly knew Psalm 108; it would have been entirely characteristic of him to use it as a morning prayer:

My heart is ready, O God,
my heart is ready!
I will sing, I will sing praises!
Awake, my soul!
Awake, O harp and lyre!
I will awake the dawn! (Psalm 108:1-2 RSV, 1st ed.)

Jeremiah did not resolve to stick it out for twenty-three years, no matter what; he got up every morning with the sun. The day was God's day, not the people's. He didn't get up to face rejection, he got up to meet with God. He didn't rise to put up with another round of mockery, he rose to be with his Lord. That is the secret of his persevering pilgrimage—not thinking with dread about the long road ahead but greeting the present moment, every present moment, with obedient delight, with expectant hope: "My heart is ready!"

We all know people who spend a lifetime at the same job, or the same marriage, or the same profession, who are slowly, inexorably diminished in the process. They are persistent in the sense that they keep doing the same thing for many years, but we don't particularly admire them for it. If anything, we feel sorry for them for having got stuck in such an uninteresting rut with neither the energy nor imagination to get out.

But we don't feel sorry for Jeremiah. He was not stuck in a rut; he was committed to a purpose. The one thing that Jeremiah shows no evidence of is bored drudgery. Everything we know of him shows that after the twenty-three years his imagination is even more alive and his spirit even more resilient than it was in his youth. He wasn't putting in his time. Every day was a new episode in the adven-

ture of living the prophetic life. The days added up to a life
of incredible tenacity, of amazing stamina.

Joel Henderson was once asked how he had managed to
write all those books. He replied that he had never written
a book. All he did was write one page a day. With his limited
energy and restricted imagination, a page at a time was all
that he could manage. But when a year was up he had a
365-page book.

Jeremiah's persistent faithfulness contrasts with the erratic and impulsive nature of the people with whom he
lived. They were full of projects, wild with enthusiasms,
but nothing ever added up. They were like a character in a
John Fowles short story—"he wanted Everest in a day; if it
took two, he lost interest."[4]

Jeremiah does his best to show them the shabby emptiness of such lives. In a bold, sexually explicit metaphor, he
captures their attention and then dramatizes the futility of
their days.

> Look at your way in the valley;
>   know what you have done—
> a restive young camel interlacing her tracks,
>   a wild ass used to the wilderness,
> in her heat sniffing the wind!
>   Who can restrain her lust? (Jer 2:23-24)

That is strong speech. Stand on a hill and look down in
the valley at a young camel looking for a mate, back and
forth, up and down. The record of her restless searching
is in the footprints in the dust. All that movement and not
going anywhere. Or look at the wild ass in heat out in the
wilderness, sniffing the wind for the scent of a mate—no
matter who—unrestrained and purposeless except for one
thing, the satisfaction of desire.

That is what you look like, preaches Jeremiah. Dominated
by appetite and impulse, your lives are empty of commitment, purpose, continuity. You are frantic and busy, rush-

ing here and there, wherever there is the slightest suggestion that you might satisfy something or other. But you
are not camels and donkeys in the rutting season; you are
persons with a capacity for faithfulness. Isn't it time to start
living like it?

Israel had a long history of unfaithfulness. Every attrac-
tively packaged promise distracted her from her God.
Every new fad was taken up and tried in a burst of short-
lived enthusiasm. For centuries it had been one lover after
another.

In another sermon to the same effect Jeremiah used a
different image: "How lightly you gad about, changing
your way! You shall be put to shame by Egypt as you were
put to shame by Assyria" (Jer 2:36). Here he holds a mirror
up to them, and they see the reflection of a fickle schoolgirl
with a crush on the new boy who has just moved in down the
street. All aflutter she can think of nothing but seeing him,
attracting his attention, getting noticed. When she is jilted
by him, she goes after the boy in the next block and the
story begins all over again. Giddy and flirtatious, the girl
flits from one boy to another, careless of all relationships,
concerned only with making an impression. And the boys,
of course, are only interested in using her. They deserve
each other.

The message is clear enough. First you had a crush on
Assyria and that was a waste. Now you have a crush on
Egypt and that will turn out the same way. If you ever
grow up, you will look back on those times in embarrassment and blush. Meanwhile God is loving you. And you
once said you loved him! Your actions develop out of your
silly fantasies. They have no basis in reality. Assyria never
cared for you; Egypt will never care for you. *God* cares
for you. And God will not permit the people he loves and
the people he created for glory to live in such silliness and
emptiness.

New Every Morning

Where did Jeremiah learn his persistence? How did he get the word into his vocabulary, into his life? Certainly not by observing the people around him. He learned it from God.

Jeremiah learned to live persistently toward God because God lived persistently toward him. The five poem-prayers in Lamentations (written in the tradition of Jeremiah) express the suffering God's people experienced during and after the fall of Jerusalem, the most devastating disaster in their history. At the very center of this dark time, and placed at almost the exact center of these five poems that lament the sin and suffering, there is this verse: "The steadfast love of the LORD never ceases, his mercies never come to an end; they are new every morning; great is thy faithfulness" (Lam 3:22-23).

There it is—"new every morning . . . great is thy faithfulness." God's persistence is not a dogged repetition of duty. It has all the surprise and creativity, and yet all the certainty and regularity, of a new day. Sunrise—when the spontaneous and the certain arrive at the same time.

Does anyone ever get used to daybreak? Every night we are "dissolved into darkness as we shall one day be dissolved into dust; our very selves, so far as we know, have been wiped out of the world of living things; and then we are raised alive like Lazarus, and found all our limbs and senses unaltered, with the coming of the day."[5] We never get used to it. Daybreak is always a surprise. There are times, of course, when we fail to respond. But when that happens we instinctively know that it is due to a deficiency within ourselves, whether from disease or depression. If the repetitions in nature are never boring, how much less the repetitions in God.

That is the source of Jeremiah's living persistence, his creative constancy. He was up before the sun, listening to God's word. Rising early, he was quiet and attentive before his Lord. Long before the yelling started, the mocking, the complaining, there was this centering, discovering, exploring time with God.

"But," Jeremiah said, "*you* have not listened. . . . *You* never listened or paid the slightest attention" (Jer 25:3-4, Bright's translation). Here, then, is the clue to our erratic life patterns, our inconstancy, our unfaithfulness, our stupid inability to distinguish between fashion and faith: we don't rise up early and listen to God. We don't daily find a time apart from the crowd, a time of silence and solitude, for preparing for the day's journey. "A very original man," says Garry Wills, "must shape his life, make a schedule that allows him to reflect, and study, and create."[6]

Jeremiah had a defined priority: persistently rising early, he listened to God, then spoke and acted what he heard. It was not because there were no other options open to him. It was not because he couldn't think of anything else to do. He had chosen what Jesus called "the one thing needful"— listening, attentively and believingly, to God.

The mark of a certain kind of genius is the ability and energy to keep returning to the same task relentlessly, imaginatively, curiously, for a lifetime. Never give up and go on to something else; never get distracted and be diverted to something else. Augustine wrote fifteen commentaries on the book of Genesis. He began at the beginning and was never satisfied that he had got to the beginning. He never felt that he had got to the depths of the first book of the Bible, down to the very origins of life, the first principles of God's ways with us. He kept returning to those first questions. Beethoven composed sixteen string quartets because he was never satisfied with what he had done. The quartet form intrigued and challenged him. Perfection eluded him—he kept coming back to it over and over in an attempt at mastery. We think he did pretty well with them, but he didn't think so. So he persisted, bringing fresh, creative energy to each day's attempt. The same thing over and over, and yet it is never the same thing, for each venture is resplendent with dazzling creativity.

And Jeremiah: "For twenty-three years . . . the word of the LORD has come to me, and I have spoken *persistently* to you." There is only one thing needful. And there is only today in which to do it. Do it. Then do it again. And again. *Persistently*. Not mindlessly, but with all the exuberance of an encore.

10 Take a Scroll and Write on It

This word came to Jeremiah from the LORD: "Take a scroll and write on it all the words that I have spoken to you against Israel and Judah and all the nations, from the day I spoke to you, from the days of Josiah until today. It may be that the house of Judah will hear all the evil which I intend to do to them, so that every one may turn from his evil way, and that I may forgive their iniquity and their sin."

Then Jeremiah called Baruch the son of Neriah, and Baruch wrote upon a scroll at the dictation of Jeremiah all the words of the LORD which he had spoken to him.

Jeremiah 36:1-4

Some people may wonder: why was the light of God given in the form of language? How is it conceivable that the divine should be contained in such brittle vessels as consonants and vowels? This question betrays the sin of our age: to treat lightly the ether which carries the light-waves of the spirit. What else in the world is as capable of bringing man and man together over the distances in space and in time? Of all things on earth, words alone never die. They have so little matter and so much meaning.... God took these Hebrew words and breathed into them of His power, and the words became a live wire charged with His spirit. To this very day they are hyphens between heaven and earth. What other medium could have been employed to convey the divine? Pictures enameled on the moon? Statues hewn out of the Rockies?

Abraham Heschel[1]

In a letter Franz Kafka wrote, "If the book we are reading does not wake us, as with a fist hammering on our skull, why then do we read it? . . . A book must be like an ice-axe to break the sea frozen inside us."[2] There are two ice-axe books in Jeremiah's life, the one he read and the one he wrote.

The Ice Axe of Deuteronomy

The book Jeremiah read was Deuteronomy. Discovered in the course of the temple repairs, it was the handbook for Josiah's reform. Jeremiah grew up with the book. He pondered and absorbed its message. He didn't read the book as a scholar, analyzing and explaining it (although it is unlikely he would reject such concerns); he didn't read the book as a reformer, searching for the principles that could be applied to society to make it whole (although he participated in such search and application); he read it as a person addressed personally by God. Everything that Jeremiah preached and later wrote shows the influence of what he read. George Adam Smith wrote that "Jeremiah heard in the heart of Deuteronomy the call of God [and] uttered his Amen to it."[3] Three elements stand out in his reading.

Reading Deuteronomy Jeremiah acquired a memory. Deuteronomy recapitulates the totality of what it means to be a people of God. Written in the form of an address by Moses on the border between wilderness and promised land, it recollects the experience of being saved out of Egypt, preserved in the wilderness and promised a life of blessing. It collects the scattered and half-remembered experiences of the past and integrates them into the present. Life is more than the diary jottings of harassed individuals: there is pattern, every detail is part of the design. Daily life in constant flight from its origin is returned to its source in this act of recollection.

Reading Deuteronomy Jeremiah developed a theology. He learned to think of God in a comprehensive, ordered, relational way. Deuteronomy presents God in a loyal, committed relationship of love with his people. God is not a random thought. God is not a word to fill in the gaps of what we don't know. God is actively, energetically dealing with people in love. *Love* is the key and characteristic word in the book.[4] This love is both God's character and his command. Because we are under this kind of God, there is no living worth the name that is not a participation in that love.

Reading Deuteronomy Jeremiah became responsible. Deuteronomy is full of commands. A command is a word that calls us to live beyond what we presently understand or feel or want. "The commandment pulls people up from animality to humanity."[5] Life is not mechanistically determined. We are not swept along in sociological movements, fixed on economic grids. Everyone has choices to make. The choices are not trial-and-error guesses; they are informed by the commands of God. These commands do not restrict a natural freedom; they create the conditions of freedom. The first word addressed to Adam by his Creator is a command (Gen 1:28). Commands assume freedom and encourage response. Addressed by commands we are trained in response-ability.

The Ice Axe of Jeremiah
The book Jeremiah read developed into the book that Jeremiah wrote. Just as Deuteronomy *repreached* the message of Moses to a people who had lost touch with Moses, so Jeremiah *repreached* the message of Deuteronomy to a people who had drifted from its moorings. Josiah, the king with whom Jeremiah grew up and shared a life shaped by the book of Deuteronomy, was dead, killed in a battle at

Megiddo. His son was on the throne and showed no sign that he had so much as heard of the book of Deuteronomy. Descent into laxity and corruption was swift. The Deuteronomy-inspired reform was in shreds.

"There is no other institution that suffers from time so much as religion," wrote Charles Williams. "At the moment when it is remotely possible that a whole generation might have learned something both of theory and practice, the learners and their learning are removed by death, and the Church is confronted with the necessity of beginning all over again. The whole labour of regenerating mankind has to begin again every thirty years or so."[6] In this case, it was seventeen years.

Jeremiah was directed: "Take a scroll and write on it all the words that I have spoken. . . . It may be that the house of Judah will hear all the evil which I intend to do to them, so that every one may turn from his evil way, and that I may forgive their iniquity and their sin" (Jer 36:2-3). God has something to say, and he wants us to know what it is. He is not secretive, delighting in keeping us in the dark; he reveals. He reveals in a form that is accessible to us: *take a scroll*—the word is to be written on everyday material, parchment or papyrus, the same kind of material we use for sending thank-you notes and making up shopping lists. Then the process is outlined: *write* develops into *hear* which develops into *turn* which develops into *forgive*.

Another book of Scripture is brought into existence. But this Scripture is not now a static phenomenon, a thing that we can handle at our pleasure or for our pleasure. It is a vortex of swiftly moving energies constituted by these five verbs *(take, write, hear, turn, forgive)*. This vortex makes God's words visible and audible and draws human life into responsiveness. Abraham Heschel, a man great in learning and prayer, complained that some people hail the Bible as literature as if that were the highest praise they could give

it, "as if 'literature' were the climax of spiritual reality."
Then he commented: "What would Moses, what would
Jeremiah have said to such praise? Perhaps the same as Ein-
stein would have said, if the manuscript of his Theory of
Relativity were acclaimed for its beautiful handwriting."[7]

Jeremiah enlisted his friend Baruch in the work. Baruch
wrote as Jeremiah dictated what he had been preaching
and praying for twenty-three years: life-probing words,
brilliant images, biting confrontations, profound analysis.
His language, as described by George Adam Smith, is
"terse, concrete, poignant and graceful."[8]

We live on the gossip of the moment and the rumors of
the hour. It is not as if we never hear the truth at all, but we
don't realize its overwhelming significance. It is an extra,
an aside. We have no sense of continuity. We respond to
whims, sometimes good, sometimes bad. Then Scripture is
placed before us. Words are assembled and arranged, and
powerful patterns of truth become visible. The sermon
that moved us to repentance ten years ago but then was
forgotten in the press of business, the prayer that lifted us
to new hope at a time of crisis but has since been buried
under failures and disappointments—these words, along
with many others that we had never known before, come
before us in such a way that everything becomes coherent
in their presence. Amnesia is replaced by recognition. Distraction is gathered into attention. Jeremiah dictates.
Baruch writes. The syntax gives shape and the metaphors
give focus to God's word.

A Word in Crisis
Several months later the Babylonian armies were in the
land, and news arrived that they had reduced the coast city
of Ashkelon to rubble. The world powers, Egypt and Babylon, were at each other's throats. In the rapid shifts of
power that were taking place, Jerusalem was dangerously

vulnerable. The people feared that their lives were up for grabs in the contest between the great powers. A day of fasting was called in response to the crisis. The city was thronged with anxious and praying people.

The timing was propitious. The sense of crisis had drawn the nation to its knees before God; the largest congregation Jeremiah would ever get was assembled in the city. Though he himself was forbidden to speak in public (he was persona non grata to King Jehoiakim),[9] his message was now written so that it could be delivered by another. Baruch took the scroll to the temple and read it out before the people (Jer 36:4-10).

Micaiah, a young man in the congregation, heard Baruch read from Jeremiah's scroll and became a true listener. He had heard Jeremiah's words many times; now he heard *God's* word. He acted swiftly. He ran to his father and told him what he had heard. His father, a member of the king's cabinet, was meeting at that moment with four other government officials. They responded to the youth's urgency and sent for Baruch to come and read the scroll to them. Baruch came and read. The father was as impressed as his son had been. His associates were likewise moved. "When they heard all the words, they turned one to another in fear; and they said to Baruch, 'We must report all these words to the king' " (Jer 36:16).

They had heard the truth and were committed to it. They were responsible men and knew that their lives and the life of the nation were addressed by this word of God. And they knew that the king must be told. They also knew their king. The moment that he heard what had been written and read, Jeremiah and Baruch were as good as dead. They advised Jeremiah and Baruch to go into hiding. The king had already murdered one prophet, Uriah, who had dared confront him (Jer 26:20-33); he wouldn't hesitate to kill another.

Scripture's task is to tell people, at the risk of their displeasure, the mystery of God and the secrets of their own hearts—to speak out and make a clean breast. There are many ways to say and write these truths: in oracles, in poems, in novels, in sermons, in satire, in journalism, in drama. Honestly written and courageously presented words reveal reality and expose our selfish attempts to violate beauty, manipulate goodness and dominate people, all the while defying God. Most of us most of the time, whether consciously or not, live this way. Honest writing shows us how badly we are living and how good life is. Enlightenment is not without pain. But the pain, accepted and endured is not a maiming but a purging. "Every significant utterance is a wound, but 'faithful are the wounds of a friend.' "[10]

The Burning of the Scroll

Now it was the king's turn to hear the scroll read. The king was in his winter room, specially constructed for the cold months (it was December), and there was a brazier of coals near him at which he was keeping himself warm. He sent a servant, Jehudi, to get the scroll and read it. The king had a penknife in his hand. When Jehudi had read three or four columns, the king, sneering and contemptuous, cut them off with his knife and tossed them into the fire. The smart-set advisors with whom he had surrounded himself joined in the joking and jeering. They all thought it was hilarious. The senior cabinet ministers who had called the king's attention to the scroll begged him to take what he heard seriously. The king was unreachable. The scroll was read and destroyed, column by column cut into strips and burned in the fire.

As this story unfolds before us we become aware of the contrast between son and father. Seventeen years before, the father, Josiah, was presented with a scroll by the state official Shaphan, and he asked that it be read aloud to him. His reaction was penitential—"he rent his clothes." He recognized the scroll as God's word and realized the sin in which they all had been ignorantly living. A prophetess, Huldah, responded to his repentant faith, "Because your heart was penitent, and you humbled yourself before the LORD, when you heard how I spoke, . . . I also have heard you, says the LORD" (2 Kings 22:19).

Now a generation later the scenario is repeated. Josiah's son, Jehoiakim, is presented with a scroll by Shaphan's son, Gemariah. Jehoiakim's reaction is also emotional, but in him it is the emotion of derision. Instead of tearing his garments in penitence as his father had, he tore up the book in ridicule. There is also a prophetic word to conclude the narration, but in contrast to the commendation of Huldah there is the condemnation of Jeremiah: "You have burned this scroll. . . . Therefore thus says the LORD concerning Jehoiakim king of Judah. . . . His dead body shall be cast out to the heat by day and the frost by night" (Jer 36:29-30). The heat the scroll had radiated as he had warmed himself at its burning wouldn't last long—he would soon be a corpse, exposed to the "frost by night"!

The key word of commendation to Josiah was "you heard how I spoke"; the key word of condemnation to Jehoiakim and his offspring was "they would not hear" (Jer 36:31). The father heard the word of God and obeyed it; the result was a surging new lease on life for the nation. The son heard the word of God and burlesqued it; the result was a precipitous fall into exile.

A Charade of Nonchalance
Jehoiakim's response to the reading of Scripture betrays excessive anxiety. Giggling in the presence of the holy, cheap joke making in the atmosphere of the sublime are defenses against an awareness that requires a change of life.

He was trying desperately to keep the truth of Jeremiah's words and the reality of God's truth at bay. But the extravagant inappropriateness of his behavior shows that it was not out of simple ignorance that he was being silly, but out of a complex selfishness. Jehoiakim knew that he was hearing the word of God; but if he gave any indication he knew, he would be accountable for responding in obedience. So he gave an elaborate charade of nonchalance, casually and indifferently whittling away at the scroll, feeding the fire with the parings until it was gone.

Jehoiakim with his penknife is a parody of all who attempt to *use* Scripture, who attempt to bring it under control and reduce it to something manageable. Scripture cannot be *used*. It is God's word calling us to a personal response. The word of God addresses us, calls us into being. The only appropriate response is a reverent answering. It is always more than we are, always previous to us, always over us.

Wanting to maintain control over our lives, to keep the initiative in our own hands, we chop the word of God into little pieces so that we can control it and maybe even put it to practical use—like warming us on a cold winter day! We reduce Scripture to something impersonal that we can use for our purposes or discard at our pleasure. We dismember its organically developed parts so that it is no longer a complete representation of God's address to us to which we must respond.

Scripture can be burned, but God's word cannot be destroyed. It has been thrown into the fire many times, but no one has yet successfully suppressed it. Jeremiah and Baruch simply went back to work again, dictating and writing. This time there was more: "And many similar words were added to them" (Jer 36:32).[11] Jehoiakim should have left well enough alone; now copies more extensive than the first edition were circulating through the shops and streets of Jerusalem.

I enjoy conversations that open with the gambit, "If you were shipwrecked on a desert island, what single book would you most like to have?" I usually try to exclude the Bible from the answers to prevent pious cheating. In the answers I like to think that I can discern significant values and tastes. The person who chooses Shakespeare's *King Lear*, I think, is probably committed to an exploration of the depths of human relationships. A choice of the *Almanac* or the *Guinness Book of World Records* shows a mind that reduces all knowledge to impersonal information, preferring to get along with as little personal relationship as possible. A preference for Milton's *Paradise Lost* indicates a bent for theological meditation. The best answer to the question that I have ever heard was the surprising, but obvious, Butler's *Practical Guide to Boat-Building*.

The book that Jeremiah read and the book that Jeremiah wrote are both boat-building kinds of books. They are not pious books of meditation. They are not about ideas or about things, but about survival—getting back home. They show how a life is constructed that gets us where we are supposed to be, to God. All of Scripture is similarly written. *Deuteronomy* was used to rebuild a society that had been shipwrecked by Manasseh's evil reign. *Jeremiah* was used to rebuild lives that suffered the shipwreck of exile. Along with the sixty-four other books that have been added to them, they continue to present the word of God to shipwrecked people and to construct a way of salvation.

11 House of the Rechabites

"Go to the house of the Rechabites, and speak with them, and bring them to the house of the LORD . . ."

"We have obeyed the voice of Jonadab the son of Rechab, our father, in all that he commanded us, to drink no wine all our days, ourselves, our wives, our sons, or our daughters, and not to build houses to dwell in. We have no vineyard or field or seed; but we have lived in tents, and have obeyed and done all that Jonadab our father commanded us."

"The sons of Jonadab the son of Rechab have kept the command which their father gave them, but this people has not obeyed me."

Jeremiah 35:2, 8-10, 16

It is more than ever the task of the little teams and small flocks, to struggle most effectively for man and the spirit, and, in particular, to give the most effective witness to those truths for which men so desperately long and which are, at present, in such short supply. For only the little teams and small flocks are able to muster around something which completely escapes technique and the process of massification, and which is the love of wisdom and of the intellect and the trust in the invisible radiation of this love. Such invisible rays carry far; they have the same kind of incredible power in the realm of the spirit that atomic fission and the miracles of microphysics have in the world of matter.

Jacques Maritain[1]

Crowds lie. The more people, the less truth.[2] Integrity is not strengthened by multiplication. We can test this observation easily. Which promise is most likely to be kept: the promise spoken by a politician to a crowd of ten thousand or the promise exchanged between two friends?

Since we all have everyday experience of the unreliability of crowds to discern and reflect the truth, it is puzzling that the appeal to numbers continues to carry so much weight with us. The selling of a million copies of a book is accepted as evidence that the book is excellent and important. The engagement of a majority of people in a certain moral behavior is set forth as evidence of its legitimacy. Approval by the masses is accreditation. But a rudimentary knowledge of history corroborated by a few moments of personal reflection will convince us that truth is not statistical and that crowds are more often foolish than wise. In crowds the truth is flattened to fit a slogan. Not only the truth that is spoken but the truth that is lived is reduced and distorted by the crowd. The crowd makes spectators of us, passive in the presence of excellence or beauty. The crowd makes consumers of us, inertly taking in whatever is pushed at us. As spectators and consumers the central and foundational elements of our being human—our ability to create, our drive to excel, our capacity to commune with God—atrophy.

There is nothing wrong, of course, in being in a crowd, and often it is unavoidable. If I want to watch some highly skilled athletes play a game and 50,000 other people also want to watch, I can hardly avoid being in a crowd, nor does it damage my life. But if in addition to watching the game I parrot the profanity of the crowd and imitate the behavior of the crowd (because 50,000 people must be right), then my life is falsified.

We cannot avoid being in crowds. Can we keep from
being crowd-conditioned? Can we keep from trading our
name in for a number, from letting the crowd reduce us
to mindless passivity?

Uncrowd-conditioned

Jeremiah dealt with crowds most of his life. Unlike many
of the prophets who were men of the desert, solitary and
rustic, Jeremiah was a man of the city "where cross the
crowded ways of life." Daily he walked its streets. Frequently he assembled in the temple courts. But while Jeremiah was often in crowds he was not crowd-conditioned.
The crowd did not dictate his message. The crowd did not
shape his values. Jeremiah did not commission a public
opinion survey to find out what the Jerusalem crowds
wanted to hear about God. He did not ask for a show of
hands to determine what level of moral behavior to stress.

God shaped his behavior. God directed his life. God
trained his perceptions. This shaping and directing and
training took place as he listened to God and spoke to God.
He meditated long and passionately on the word of God;
he forged responses that were absolutely and intensely
personal. Everything he lived and spoke issued from this
inner action: "There is in my heart as it were a burning
fire shut up in my bones, and I am weary with holding it
in, and I cannot" (Jer 20:9).

Jeremiah made his mark. He wanted everything God
promises. He wanted to participate in all that God does. His
spiritual intensity and prophetic passion set him apart. He
became what Søren Kierkegaard, himself a strikingly Jere-
miah-like figure, called, "the single one, the individual."[3]

Sometimes in the presence of a person of surpassing excellence we are stimulated to strive for a similar achievement. We see an athlete perform and decide to embrace
the disciplines that will give poise and grace to our lives.

We hear an artist play and determine never to be content with anything sloppy or ugly in our lives again. We observe a person live with courage and zest and decide that we also will pursue the very best that is in us. But other times we respond by being intimidated. We assume that no matter how much we try we could never approximate such a life. Our inadequacies are exposed in the comparison and we accommodate ourselves to getting along and getting by. The artist, the athlete and the saint are rejected as evidence and proof of what is possible and treated as diversions and entertainments for lazy spectators and bored consumers.[4]

This was Jeremiah's fate in Jerusalem. The crowd avoided dealing with his life by setting him apart. The crowds understood what he was saying and probably admired the way he was living, but their self-concepts were crowd-conditioned. They didn't disbelieve in God, but they disqualified themselves from strenuous, personal participation.

Biblical faith, however, has always insisted that there are no special aptitudes for a life with God—no required level of intelligence or degree of morality, no particular spiritual experience. The statement "I'm not the religious type" is inadmissible. There are no religious types. There are only human beings, every one created for a relationship with God that is personal and eternal.

How can people who are conditioned to a life of distraction and indulgence be moved to live at their best, to be artists of the everyday, to plunge into life and not loiter on the fringes?

The Guild of Rechabites
One day some strange people appeared on the streets of Jerusalem. They were called Rechabites. The Rechabites led a wandering life and lived in tents. They were a guild of metalworkers involved in the making of chariots and

other weaponry. They roamed the country, setting up
camp outside villages and cities. If you had a javelin that
needed straightening or a chariot wheel that needed mend-
ing, you put it aside for the time when the Rechabites would
arrive. They were a small band and kept to themselves.[5]

The Rechabites traced their ancestry back 250 years, to
one Jonadab ben Rechab in the time of Jehu. They accounted for their disciplined life and distinctive identity
in terms of their obedience to the command given by their
ancestor: "We have obeyed the voice of Jonadab the son of
Rechab, our father, in all that he commanded us, to drink
no wine all our days, ourselves, our wives, our sons, or our
daughters, and not to build houses to dwell in. We have
no vineyard or field or seed; but we have lived in tents, and
have obeyed and done all that Jonadab our father commanded us" (Jer 35:8-10).

Craftsmen in metal would have many trade secrets, tight-
ly held. The abstinence from intoxicants followed from the
well-known rule, "loose lips sink ships." Metallurgists in
antiquity, as a rule, formed proud families with long gene-
alogies. Marriages were carefully arranged within the
guild, preventing the entrance of outsiders. The smith had
to dispose of a formidable body of technical lore which was
handed down and guarded jealously from generation to
generation. The nature of his work prevented the smith
from establishing a permanent residence. He remained in
one locality from a few months to several years until the
supply of ore and fuel at that place was exhausted. The
smith's work required such skill and long practice that
agricultural work was excluded.

The Babylonian invasion of Judah had made living in
the country dangerous and so the Rechabites had come
inside the city walls of Jerusalem for safety. They were an
oddity in the city, conspicuous in their strangeness. They
were, of course, noticed, commented on, gawked at. Within

two or three days everyone would either have seen them or heard about them.

An Invitation to Lunch

Then this: "The word which came to Jeremiah from the LORD: . . . 'Go to the house of the Rechabites, and speak with them, and bring them to the house of the LORD, into one of the chambers; then offer them wine to drink' " (Jer 35:1-2).

But Rechabites don't drink wine. Everybody knows that. Why invite them to a wine party that they can't enjoy? Then it dawned on Jeremiah. Of course. The Rechabites were living evidence, right on the crowded streets of Jerusalem, of the two things the crowd-conditioned people assumed were impossible: They were evidence that everyday, ordinary people could live their entire lives directed by a personal command (and not the impersonal pressures of the crowd); they were evidence that it is possible to maintain persistently a distinctive way of life (and not assimilate to the fashions of the crowd). The people had already noticed the Rechabites—how could they miss them!—now if they could just be made to notice exactly what it was that set them apart and gave them their identity, then they themselves might realize that a personal identity and a disciplined distinctiveness were possible for them also.

Jeremiah saw the possibilities and went to work. He arranged for the use of a public room in the temple precincts —an open chamber where they would be seen both by the religious leaders and by the general populace. He invited the Rechabites—there couldn't have been very many, perhaps fifteen or twenty—for a luncheon. He placed pitchers of wine and large drinking bowls on the table.

A Disciplined People

Jeremiah was no novice at this business of using experiences from the streets in order to get people to pay atten-

tion to God. One day in the bazaar he had bought a fine
linen garment, the kind worn for a wedding ceremony or a
religious festival. I always imagine Jeremiah making a pro-
duction out of the purchase, spending most of an afternoon
bargaining with the shopkeeper (not in itself an unusual
practice in the Middle East) so that a lot of people would
know of the purchase. The word would get around: "What
is Jeremiah buying that fine linen garment for? What
special event is coming up? What was he invited to that we
weren't?"

Then Jeremiah made a show of wadding up this beautiful piece of clothing and sticking it in a rock crevice to keep
it safe until the time that he was going to wear it. Later he
went back to retrieve it, as if to wear it for the special
occasion. It was rotten, in tatters because of exposure to
the elements and the insects.

The people got the message: Israel was the fine garment
that God wanted to wear, but she wasn't ready yet to be
used for his purposes. She wanted to live an ordinary life
first, so she wadded herself up and stuffed herself into the
secure routines, separating herself from what God had at
great cost purchased her for. But when that day comes it
will turn out that she is good for nothing. The beautiful
moral life that she set aside for a more convenient day will
turn out, when she picks it up, to be mildewed and moth-
eaten (Jer 13).

Another time Jeremiah staggered through the streets of
Jerusalem with an ox yoke on his shoulders, telling the
people that they were going to experience just such servi-
tude under the approaching Babylonian rule, and that they
should get used to the idea for it was far better than getting
killed (Jer 27-28).

This day it was the talk-of-the-town Rechabites that Jeremiah used. Invited by Jeremiah, they were now at table with
him. The wine was on the table. Jeremiah, a gracious and

friendly host, lifted his glass in a toast: *L'Chaim!* Drink wine!

Did they join in? Did they relax their rule for the moment so as not to offend their new friend? Did they realize that they were living under emergency war conditions and that it was only courteous to adapt to the customs of their protectors? Did they take a realistic view of the situation and share the common cup, showing appreciation for being treated so generously?

They did not, as Jeremiah knew they would not. "They answered, 'We will drink no wine, for Jonadab the son of Rechab, our father, commanded us, "You shall not drink wine" ' " (Jer 35:6). The Rechabites lived life not on the basis of what was current with the crowd but on the basis of what had been commanded by their ancestor. Their way of life was not formed out of historical conditions but out of centuries of devotion. The ancient command, not the current headline, gave them their identity. That word shaped and preserved their proud traditions as skilled craftsmen. Neither the hospitality of a kind host nor the customs of the city where they had come for sanctuary could distract them from what was essential: that they were a commanded people, that they were a disciplined people. Jonadab's 250-year-old command carried far more weight with them than Jeremiah's immediate friendship. The discipline that made it possible for them to maintain their craft was far more important to them than making the commonsense adaptations that would have given them an easy rapport with their new neighbors.

Life in Relationship to God

Now Jeremiah had both his text and the attention of the crowds: "Will you not receive instruction and listen to my words? says the LORD. The command which Jonadab the son of Rechab gave to his sons, to drink no wine, has been kept; and they drink none to this day, for they have obeyed their father's command. I have spoken to you persistently, but you have not listened to me. . . . The sons of Jonadab the son of Rechab have kept the command which their father gave them, but this people has not obeyed me" (Jer 35:13-14, 16).

Note well that Jeremiah did not say, "You must sell your houses and live in tents; you must abandon your vineyards and roam the desert; you must abstain from wine and drink only water." It was not the specific details of the Rechabite life that were held up but that they lived in obedience to a command and lived with integrity in a discipline.

The essence of Jeremiah's message here is this: "You also have a father who has commanded you to live in total relationship to him. You know that he has set you apart for a life of love. Why don't you live in response to it? If you think it is because ordinary, mortal human beings can't do it, think again. The Rechabites are ordinary, mortal human beings, and they have been doing it for 250 years. You also have a way of life that requires certain disciplines to maintain its character. The disciplines involve you in making specific decisions about the way you live: regular worship, faithful prayer, tithing and caring for the poor, moral conduct and the pursuit of righteousness. Now, why don't you do it? If you think that is too rigorous a life for ordinary, mortal human beings, think again. The Rechabites are ordinary, mortal human beings, and they have been doing it for 250 years.

Don't just look at them. Don't just talk about them. Pay attention to what is distinctive about them. They are not entertainment, they are example. Let them show you how badly and boringly you live—and how well you can live.[6] Your problem is not that you are incapable but that you are lazy. There is not a single person in Jerusalem who is not up to living consciously and deliberately as a child of God, and then practicing the distinctive disciplines that support and preserve a life of faith. But you have let the crowd turn you into spectators and consumers. You have let your lives get flabby and indulgent. You have ignored the best things that have ever been said to you—God's word!—and let the chatter and gossip of the crowd fill your ears. You have abandoned the simple actions that people of faith have used for centuries to keep in touch with the truth of God, the beauty of creation and the reality of being human. Instead you have let the crowd distract you with frivolities and dehumanize you with propaganda.

Why will you not let God's command develop in you a life of holy obedience instead of letting the crowd drag you into a sloppy indolence? "The sons of Jonadab the son of Rechab have kept the command which their father gave them, but this people has not obeyed me."

Larger but Smaller
Jeremiah raises weighty objections to our unreflective ways of going about our well-defined jobs, jobs that become lives shaped and sanctioned by the crowd. The New York philosopher William Barrett objects: "Modern civilization has raised the material level of millions of people beyond the expectations of the past, has it succeeded in making people happier? To judge by the bulk of modern literature, we would have to answer 'No'; and in some respects we might even have to say it has accomplished the reverse."[7]

The moral level of our society is shameful. The spiritual integrity of our culture is an embarrassment. Any part of our lives that is turned over to the crowd makes it and us worse. The larger the crowd, the smaller our lives. Pliny the Elder once said that the Romans, when they couldn't make a building beautiful, made it big. The practice continues to be popular: If we can't do it well, we make it larger. We add dollars to our income, rooms to our houses, activities to our schedules, appointments to our calendars. And the quality of life diminishes with each addition.

On the other hand, every time that we retrieve a part of our life from the crowd and respond to God's call to us, we are that much more ourselves, more human. Every time we reject the habits of the crowd and practice the disciplines of faith, we become a little more alive.

12 Letter to the Exiles

Thus says the LORD of hosts, the God of Israel, to all the exiles whom I have sent into exile from Jerusalem to Babylon: Build houses and live in them; plant gardens and eat their produce. Take wives and have sons and daughters. . . . Seek the welfare of the city where I have sent you into exile, and pray to the LORD on its behalf, for in its welfare you will find your welfare. . . . Do not let your prophets and your diviners who are among you deceive you, and do not listen to the dreams which they dream, for it is a lie which they are prophesying to you in my name; I did not send them, says the LORD. . . .

For I know the plans I have for you, says the LORD, plans for welfare and not for evil, to give you a future and a hope. Then you will call upon me and come and pray to me, and I will hear you. You will seek me and find me; when you seek me with all your heart, I will be found by you, says the LORD.

Jeremiah 29:4-14

Christ is certainly no less concerned than Nietzsche that the personality should receive the fullest development of which it is capable, and be more and more of a power. The difference between them lies in the moral method by which the personality is put into possession of itself and its resources—in the one case by asserting self, in the other by losing it. . . . We com-

plete our personality only as we fall into place and service in the vital movement of the society in which we live. Isolation means arrested development. The aggressive egotist is working his own moral destruction by stunting and shrinking his true personality. Social life, duty, and sympathy are the only conditions under which a true personality can be shaped. And if it be asked how a society so crude, imperfect, unmoral, and even immoral as that in which we live is to mould a personality truly moral, it is here that Christ comes to the rescue with the gift to faith both of an active Spirit and of a society complete in Himself.

Peter T. Forsyth[1]

Exile is traumatic and terrifying. Our sense of who we are is very much determined by the place we are in and the people we are with. When that changes, violently and abruptly, who are we? The accustomed ways we have of finding our worth and sensing our significance vanish. The first wave of emotion recedes and leaves us feeling worthless, meaningless. We don't fit anywhere. No one expects us to do anything. No one needs us. We are extra baggage. We aren't necessary.

Israel was taken into exile in 587 B.C.[2] The people were uprooted from the place in which they were born. The land that had been promised to them, which they had possessed, in which their identity as a people of God had been formed, was gone. They were forced to travel across the Middle Eastern desert seven hundred miles, leaving home, temple and hills. In the new land, Babylon, customs were strange, the language incomprehensible, and the landscape oddly flat and featureless. All the familiar landmarks were gone. The weather was different. The faces were unrecognized and unrecognizing.

Israel's exile was a violent and extreme form of what all of us experience from time to time. Inner experiences of exile take place even if we never move from the street on which we were brought up. We are exiled from the womb and begin life in strange and harsh surroundings. We are exiled from our homes at an early age and find ourselves in the terrifying and demanding world of school. We are exiled from school and have to make our way the best we can in the world of work. We are exiled from our hometowns and have to find our way in new states and cities.

These experiences of exile, minor and major, continue through changes in society, changes in government, changes in values, changes in our bodies, our emotions, our families and marriages. We barely get used to one set of circumstances and faces when we are forced to deal with another. The exile experienced by the Hebrews is a dramatic instance of what we all experience simply by being alive in this world. Repeatedly we find ourselves in circumstances where we are not at home. We are "strangers in a strange land."[3]

The essential meaning of exile is that we are where we don't want to be. We are separated from home. We are not permitted to reside in the place where we comprehend and appreciate our surroundings. We are forced to be away from that which is most congenial to us. It is an experience of dislocation—everything is out of joint; nothing fits together. The thousand details that have been built up through the years that give a sense of at-homeness—gestures, customs, rituals, phrases—are all gone. Life is ripped out of the familiar soil of generations of language, habit, weather, story-telling, and rudely and unceremoniously dropped into some unfamiliar spot of earth. The place of exile may boast a higher standard of living. It may be more pleasant in its weather. That doesn't matter. It isn't home.

But this very strangeness can open up new reality to us. An accident, a tragedy, a disaster of any kind can force the realization that the world is not predictable, that reality is far more extensive than our habitual perception of it. With the pain and in the midst of alienation a sense of freedom can occur.

False Dreams
The reason for Israel's exile is clear enough: Jeremiah and other prophets had preached that the nation's stability and security depended on a certain faithfulness to the love of God. That message had been scorned and rejected. The Babylonian army came one day and captured the city. After

conquering Jerusalem the Babylonians selected the leading people of the city for deportation. The tactic was to remove all persons of influence and leadership—artisans, merchants, political leaders—so that the general populace would be dependent on and submissive to the invaders. Without leaders the people, like sheep, would submit to the puppet king and the occupying army with a minimum of hassle. Jeremiah, interestingly, was left behind. He had been ignored for so long as a leader by his own people that the Babylonians did not consider him important enough to exile.

How did these people in exile feel? How did they respond? If we imagine ourselves in a similar situation, remembering how we respond when we are forced to spend extended time with people we don't like in a place we don't like, we will not be far from the truth. Their experience can be expressed in a complaint: "A terrible thing has happened to us. And it's not fair. I know we weren't perfect, but we were no worse than the rest of them. And here we end up in this Babylonian desert while our friends are carrying on life as usual in Jerusalem. Why us? We can't understand the language; we don't like the food; the manners of the Babylonians are boorish; the schools are sub-standard; there are no decent places to worship; the plains are barren; the weather is atrociously hot; the temples are polluted with immorality; everyone speaks with an accent." They complained bitterly about the terrible circumstances in which they were forced to live. They longed, achingly, for Jerusalem. They wallowed in self-pity, what Robertson Davies calls the "harlot emotion."[4]

They had religious leaders with them who nurtured their self-pity. We know the names of three of them: Ahab, Zedekiah and Shemiah. These prophets called attention to the unfairness of their plight and stirred the pots of discontent: "Yes, the old religion of Jerusalem is what we must get back to. Yes, it's worse luck that we are here when so many are enjoying the good life back in Jerusalem. But hang on a little longer and we'll get back. It can't last much longer. How can it? Not one of us deserves such a life. Justice will prevail." These prophets described dreams, God-given they claimed, that revealed that the exile would end soon.

These three prophets made a good living fomenting discontent and merchandising nostalgia. But their messages and dreams, besides being false, were destructive. False dreams interfere with honest living. As long as the people thought that they might be going home at any time, it made no sense to engage in committed, faithful work in Babylon. If there was a good chance that they would soon get back all they had lost, there was no need to develop a life of richness, texture and depth where they were. Since their real relationships were back in Jerusalem, they could be casual and irresponsible in their relationships in exile—they weren't going to see these people much longer anyhow. Why bother planting gardens? That is backbreaking work, and they would probably be out of there before harvest time. Why learn the business practices of the culture? That is demanding; they would get along with odd jobs here and there. Why take on the disciplines of marriage and family? They would make do with casual sexual encounters until they got back to Jerusalem where they could settle down to serious family building.

The prophets manipulated the self-pity of the people into neurotic fantasies. The people, glad for a religious reason to be lazy, lived hand to mouth, parasites on society, irresponsible in their relationships, indifferent to the reality of their actual lives.

A Letter from Jeremiah
One day two men from Jerusalem appeared unannounced

among the exiles: Elasah and Gemariah. They had come on official business, carrying a message to the king of Babylon. On their way to the palace they visited the community in exile. The air was charged with excitement. Everyone had questions: What was this one doing? What was that one doing? Elasah and Gemariah waved them silent. Before giving them the gossip they had a message from Jeremiah, a letter to the exiles.

"Thus says the LORD of hosts, the God of Israel, to all the exiles whom I have sent into exile from Jerusalem to Babylon: Build houses and live in them; plant gardens and eat their produce. Take wives and have sons and daughters. . . . Seek the welfare of the city. . . . Pray to the LORD on its behalf. . . . Do not let your prophets and your diviners who are among you deceive you, and do not listen to the dreams which they dream, for it is a lie which they are prophesying to you in my name."

Build houses and live in them. You are not camping. This is your home; make yourself at home. This may not be your favorite place, but it is a place. Dig foundations; construct a habitation; develop the best environment for living that you can. If all you do is sit around and pine for the time you get back to Jerusalem, your present lives will be squalid and empty. Your life right now is every bit as valuable as it was when you were in Jerusalem, and every bit as valuable as it will be when you get back to Jerusalem. Babylonian exile is not your choice, but it is what you are given. Build a Babylonian house and live in it as well as you are able.

Plant gardens and eat their produce. Enter into the rhythm of the seasons. Become a productive part of the economy of the place. You are not parasites. Don't expect others to do it for you. Get your hands into the Babylonian soil. Become knowledgeable about the Babylonian irrigation system. Acquire skill in cultivating fruits and vegetables in this soil and climate. Get some Babylonian recipes and cook them.

Take wives and have sons and daughters. These people among whom you are living are not beneath you, nor are they above you; they are your equals with whom you can engage in the most intimate and responsible of relationships. You cannot be the person God wants you to be if you keep yourself aloof from others. That which you have in common is far more significant than what separates you. They are God's persons: your task as a person of faith is to develop trust and conversation, love and understanding.

Seek the welfare of the city where I have sent you into exile, and pray to the LORD on its behalf, for in its welfare you will find your welfare. Welfare: *shalom.* Shalom means wholeness, the dynamic, vibrating health of a society that pulses with divinely directed purpose and surges with life-transforming love. Seek the shalom and pray for it. Throw yourselves into the place in which you find yourself, but not on its terms, on God's terms. *Pray.* Search for that center in which God's will is being worked out (which is what we do when we pray) and work from that center.

Jeremiah's letter is a rebuke and a challenge: "Quit sitting around feeling sorry for yourselves. The aim of the person of faith is not to be as comfortable as possible but to live as deeply and thoroughly as possible—to deal with the reality of life, discover truth, create beauty, act out love. You didn't do it when you were in Jerusalem. Why don't you try doing it here, in Babylon? Don't listen to the lying prophets who make an irresponsible living by selling you false hopes. You are in Babylon for a long time. You better make the best of it. Don't just get along, waiting for some miraculous intervention. Build houses, plant gardens, marry husbands, marry wives, have children, pray for the wholeness of Babylon, and do everything you can to develop that wholeness. The only place you have to be human is where you are right now. The only opportunity you will ever have to live by faith is in the circumstances you are provided this very day: this house you live in, this family you find yourself in, this job you have been given, the weather conditions that prevail at this moment."

Living at Our Best

Exile (being where we don't want to be with people we don't want to be with) forces a decision: Will I focus my attention on what is wrong with the world and feel sorry for myself? Or will I focus my energies on how I can live at my best in this place I find myself? It is always easier to complain about problems than to engage in careers of virtue. George Eliot in her novel *Felix Holt* has a brilliantly appropriate comment on this question: "Everything's wrong says he. That's a big text. But does he want to make everything right? Not he. He'd lose his text."[5]

Daily we face decisions on how we will respond to these exile conditions. We can say: "I don't like it; I want to be where I was ten years ago. How can you expect me to throw myself into what I don't like—that would be sheer hypocrisy. What sense is there in taking risks and tiring myself out among people I don't even like in a place where I have no future?"

Or we can say: "I will do my best with what is here. Far more important than the climate of this place, the economics of this place, the neighbors in this place, is the God of this place. God is here with me. What I am experiencing right now is on ground that was created by him and with people whom he loves. It is just as possible to live out the will of God here as any place else. I am full of fear. I don't know my way around. I have much to learn. I'm not sure I can make it. But I had feelings like that back in Jerusalem. Change is hard. Developing intimacy among strangers is always a risk. Building relationships in unfamiliar and hostile surroundings is difficult. But if that is what it means to be alive and human, I will do it."

Fenelon used to say that there are two kinds of people: some look at life and complain of what is not there; others look at life and rejoice in what is there.[6] Will we live on the basis of what we don't have or on what we do have?

Invitation and Promise
So much for the rebuke and counsel in Jeremiah's letter to the exiles. There is also invitation and promise in it, and this is what finally came to the center and shaped the exile experience: "I know the plans I have for you, says the LORD, plans for welfare and not for evil, to give you a future and a hope. Then you will call upon me and come and pray to me, and I will hear you. You will seek me and find me; when you seek me with all your heart, I will be found by you, says the LORD."

Jeremiah habitually used words greatly, but never more so than in these sentences.

A few people rejected the message out of hand. The three prophets, for instance, were furious. Shemiah wrote a sharp, angry letter back to the Jerusalem high priest, Zephaniah, and said, "Can't you shut up Jeremiah? How long are you going to permit this crazy man to rant and rave and write letters telling us it is going to be a long exile? Do you realize what that will do to us? If people start feeling at home in Babylon, we will *never* get home to Jerusalem! Why have you not disciplined Jeremiah of Anathoth?" (Jer 29:24-28).

But others, maybe most, accepted the message. Jarred out of their everydayness by the exile, they embarked on "the search."[7] They settled down to find out what it meant to be God's people in the place they did not want to be—in Babylon. The result was that this became the most creative period in the entire sweep of Hebrew history. They did not lose their identity, they discovered it. They learned how to pray in deeper and more life-changing ways than ever.

They wrote and copied and pondered the vast revelation that had come down to them from Moses and the prophets, and they came to recognize the incredible riches of their Scriptures. They found that God was not dependent on a place, that he was not tied to familiar surroundings. The violent dislocation of the exile shook them out of their comfortable but reality-distorting assumptions and allowed them to see depths and heights that they had never even imagined before. They lost everything that they thought was important and found what was important: they found God.

The exile tore the cover off their way of life and showed its emptiness. Never again could they live by bread alone. The word of God was essential nourishment. They realized that this extraordinary change of life could only take place in the structures of the everyday—houses and gardens, marriages and children. When Jeremiah directed them to build houses and plant gardens and raise families they did not misunderstand him to mean that they were to assimilate to Babylonia. That would be no more than to repeat the sins of Jerusalem in Babylonia. They embraced the everyday, but did not become absorbed in it. They did not let the duties and routines of life dull them: they prayed and they searched. The search paid off: they noticed the texture of life; they became responsive to the many subtleties just waiting for an eye to notice them, an ear to listen to them, a mind to find them worthy of attention.

The exile was the "crucible of Israel's faith."[8] They were pushed to the edge of existence where they thought they were hanging on by the skin of their teeth, and they found that in fact they had been pushed to the center, where God was. They experienced not bare survival but abundant life. Now they saw their previous life as subsistence living, a marginal existence absorbed in consumption and fashion, empty ritual and insensitive exploitation. Exile pushed them from the margins of life to the vortex where all the issues of life and death, love and meaning, purpose and value formed the dynamic everyday, participation-demanding realities of God's future with them.

It keeps on happening. Exile is the worst that reveals the best. "It's hard believing," says Faulkner, "but disaster seems to be good for people."[9] When the superfluous is stripped away we find the essential—and the essential is God. Normal life is full of distractions and irrelevancies. Then catastrophe: Dislocation. Exile. Illness. Accident. Job loss. Divorce. Death. The reality of our lives is rearranged without anyone consulting us or waiting for our permission. We are no longer at home.

All of us are given moments, days, months, years of exile. What will we do with them? Wish we were someplace else? Complain? Escape into fantasies? Drug ourselves into oblivion? Or build and plant and marry and seek the shalom of the place we inhabit and the people we are with? Exile reveals what really matters and frees us to pursue what really matters, which is to seek the Lord with all our hearts.

13 Sentry...King... Eunuch

When he was at the Benjamin Gate, a sentry there named Irijah the son of Shelemiah, son of Hananiah, seized Jeremiah the prophet, saying, "You are deserting to the Chaldeans."...

When Jeremiah had come to the dungeon cells, and remained there many days, King Zedekiah sent for him, and received him. The king questioned him secretly in his house, and said, "Is there any word from the LORD?"...

When Ebedmelech the Ethiopian, a eunuch, who was in the king's house, heard that they had put Jeremiah into the cistern... Ebedmelech... said to the king, "My lord the king, these men have done evil in all that they did to Jeremiah the prophet by casting him into the cistern; and he will die there of hunger."... So Ebedmelech... drew Jeremiah up with ropes and lifted him out of the cistern.

Jeremiah 37:13, 16-17; 38:7-13

I must register a certain impatience with the faddish equation, never suggested by me, of the term identity with the question, "Who am I?" This question nobody would ask himself except in a more or less transcient morbid state, in a creative self-confrontation, or in an adolescent state sometimes combining both; wherefore on occasion I find myself asking a student who claims that he is in an "identity crisis" whether he is complaining or boasting. The pertinent question, if it can be put into the first person at all, would be, "What do I want to make of myself, and what do I have to work with?"

Erik H. Erikson[1]

Most figures in history books are flashes of color that illuminate an episode and are then forgotten. How many can recall ten years back the name of the Secretary of State —certainly one of the most prestigious positions in the world? Who can name the best-selling author of five years ago? But the significance of a few persons, instead of fading, blazes more brightly each century. Their significance blazes because they did not merely fulfill a prestigious role or get associated with a notable event. They became *human* in depth and thoroughness. These few, in R. P. Blackmur's words, "show an attractive force, massive and inexhaustible, and a disseminative force which is the inexhaustible spring or constant declaration of value. Where your small man is a knoll to be smoothed away [such a person is] a mountain to be mined on all flanks."[2]

Jeremiah is a "mountain to be mined on all flanks." He centers an epoch. He was a first-hand participant in the events which became the pivot for a millennium. The age of Jeremiah is a nodal ganglion that shoots out nerve endings in all directions of human existence: philosophy, religion, politics, art. In China, India, Israel and Greece the foundations are laid for universal history. Karl Jaspers describes Jeremiah's century as the "axial time" *(Achsenzeit)*. [3]

The man made headlines. His theological perception, his religious sensibility, his rhetorical power, his emotional range, his confrontational courage—these all made their historical mark. But the primary interest of people of faith in Jeremiah is not in his historical impact but in his personal development.

Only a few people make the historical headlines, but anyone can become human. Is it possible to be great when you are taking out the garbage as well as when you are signing a

peace treaty? Is it possible to exhibit grace in your conduct
in the kitchen as well as in a nationally televised debate?

I once knew a man well who had a commanding public
presence and exuded charm to all he met. What he said
mattered. He had *influence*. He was always impeccably
dressed and unfailingly courteous. But his secretary was
frequently in tears as a result of his rudely imperious demands. Behind the scenes he was tyrannical and insensitive.
His public image was flawless; his personal relationships
were shabby.

How did Jeremiah deal with the people day by day? What
was it like to be with him when he wasn't preaching a sermon, or polishing an oracle, or waging a confrontation?
The sifted reflection of the centuries adds up to an impressive consensus: Jeremiah became human in a complex and
developed *personal* sense. An examination of some of the
persons with whom he had to do strengthens our estima-
tion of his "full humanness," Abraham Maslow's phrase for
our rarely realized destinies.[4]

In chapters 37-39 of Jeremiah decisive historical events
are taking place. World history is being shaped before our
eyes. The nation is being radically altered. Powerful theological realities are emerging. Jeremiah is in the middle of
it all. But Jeremiah, while not oblivious to the big issues,
is mostly dealing with *persons,* persons with *names.* Named
persons formed the raw material for Jeremiah's daily life
of faith. Every life of faith, whether it is conspicuous or
obscure, is worked out in the context of persons not unlike
the persons with whom Jeremiah rubbed shoulders. Quite
apart from the big ideas we ponder, the important movements we participate in, the particular jobs we are given,
named persons constitute most of the agenda of our lives.
Three men on Jeremiah's agenda are representatively significant: Irijah the sentry, Zedekiah the king, Ebedmelech
the eunuch.

Irijah the Sentry

The city was under final attack by the Babylonians. It would soon fall. Jeremiah had given counsel to the leaders and had preached to the people that the Babylonian presence was God's judgment: it should be accepted and submitted to. They had sinned and they were being judged. The judgment was God's way of restoring wholeness.

People didn't like that. They kept trying to find ways to avoid the reality of judgment, to think in other categories than those of right and wrong, sin and irresponsibility. One of their substitute ways of thinking was in terms of loyalty and disloyalty. Patriotism was used to muddle the sense of morality: "Our beloved country is being attacked and we must be loyal to it; in times of crisis it is not right to criticize your leaders. It is disloyal, an act of treachery."

Using jingoist language is far easier than taking responsibility for righteousness in the nation. Far easier to shout patriotic slogans than to work patriotically for justice.

One day Jeremiah was going out the city gate to his hometown of Anathoth, three miles away. Irijah, the sentry, arrested him on the grounds that he had caught him defecting to the enemy.

Jeremiah had lived in Jerusalem all his adult life. He had been a public figure for over thirty years. He had established credentials as a loyal friend and adviser to the great King Josiah. He had never for a moment rejected or repudiated his identity as a Jew or exempted himself from any of the obligations of membership in that community. To anyone who knew him he obviously was not a bystander criticizing and not a turncoat propagandizing, but an insider agonizing.

Irijah led the man he had arrested to his bosses, the princes, who beat him and imprisoned him. Apparently they had been waiting for any incident that they could use to pounce on him. Irijah, with the undiscriminating reflexes of a watchdog, pounced.

Irijah was a man who used his job to escape his responsibilities as a person. He was a bureaucrat in the worst sense of the word, a person who hides behind the rules and prerogatives of a job description to do work that destroys people. Without considering morality or righteousness, God or person, he did his job. We meet these people all the time. And there are more and more jobs like this all the time. Every day people are hurt and demeaned by officeholders who refuse to look us in the eye, shielding themselves behind regulations and paperwork, secretaries and committees.

Irijah was the kind of person that Melville, in his novel *The Confidence Man,* describes with great scorn as "the moderate man, the invaluable understrapper of the wicked man. You, the moderate man, may be used for wrong, but you are useless for right."[5] Irijah, no doubt, would have protested vehemently that he had nothing against Jeremiah personally, that he was just doing what he had been told to do.

The most famous twentieth-century instance of Irijah is Adolf Eichmann, key figure in the murder of six million Jews in Nazi Germany. At his trial in Jerusalem it became quite clear that he had nothing against the Jews; he was just doing his job. No great venom of hate flowed in him; he was simply being obedient to what his superiors told him. Hannah Arendt coined the phrase "the banality of evil" to describe him.[6] Incalculable evil comes from these unlikely sources: quiet, efficient, little people doing their job, long since having given up thinking of themselves as responsible, moral individuals.

Jeremiah responded to Irijah with implacable endurance. He did not bluster and curse. He did not threaten and rail. Nor was he a lifeless doormat. He asserted his innocence and he endured; he accepted this banal stupidity with, it seems, equanimity, and persisted in his vocation.

Zedekiah the King

Zedekiah was not properly the king but a puppet king appointed by the Babylonians. The actual king, Jehoiachin, had been taken into exile in 598 B.C. along with most of the ruling class of the city. His uncle, Zedekiah, was appointed to rule in his place. Zedekiah was king for eleven years. All through those eleven years he had frequent conversations with Jeremiah. Jeremiah had been closely associated with his brother, the great Josiah, and with both his nephews, the kings Jehoiakim and Jehoiachin.

Zedekiah had mixed feelings about Jeremiah. He respected him. How could he not respect him?—his stature was immense, his integrity impressive, his courage legendary. But he was also an embarrassment, for Zedekiah permitted himself to be surrounded with the usual crowd of self-serving sycophants, who were trying to gain advantage from association with his kingship. He could well guess that Jeremiah had a quiet contempt for such persons.

A weak, vacillating person, Zedekiah was appointed to rule, we suspect, because the Babylonians knew that he had no will of his own and would submit to what was commanded. What they failed to anticipate was that he would do what he was told by anyone who happened to be in the room with him. When the Babylonians were gone and ultranationalists of the most reckless sort began showing up with elaborate plots to throw off the Babylonian rule with the help of an Egyptian alliance, he was easily swayed. Sometimes he would have qualms of conscience and call Jeremiah in for a consultation and, for a brief time, pay attention to the prophetic word. But nothing lasted long with Zedekiah. The man was a marshmallow. He received impressions from anyone who pushed hard enough. When the pressure was off, he gradually resumed his earlier state ready for the next impression. In contrast to Jeremiah, who was formed from within by obedience to God and faith in

God (an iron pillar!), Zedekiah took on whatever shape the circumstances required.

Zedekiah shows that good intentions are worthless if they are not coupled with character development. We don't become whole persons by merely wanting to become whole, by consulting the right prophets, by reading the right book. Intentions must mature into commitments if we are to become persons with definition, with character, with substance.

After the princes threw Jeremiah into the dungeon at the time of his arrest by Irijah, Zedekiah secretly brought him to his palace for a conversation. Zedekiah would not do this openly for fear of the princes. But neither would he ignore him, fearing that he might not get in on an important truth that Jeremiah might provide. Later the princes, enraged at Jeremiah preaching from his prison cell, threw him into a cistern. Zedekiah did nothing to prevent it.

Zedekiah was hardly a person at all. There was nothing to him. He fit into whatever plans stronger people had for him. He was not an evil person. There is no evidence that he premeditated wrongdoing. But, and this is the significant fact, neither did he premeditate goodness. And goodness does not just happen. It does not spring full-bodied out of the head of kingly intent. It requires careful nurture, disciplined training, long development. For this, Zedekiah had no stomach.

Zedekiah must have been one of the most difficult persons in all of Jeremiah's life. One king (Josiah) had been his close friend; one king (Jehoiakim) had been his implacable enemy. But this king was formless: he could never be counted on for anything, whether positive or negative. Meanwhile Jeremiah maintained his witness under the faithfulness of his God, quite apart from the fickleness of his king.

Ebedmelech the Eunuch

Ebedmelech was a foreigner, a black man from Ethiopia and an official in the administrative government. When he learned that Jeremiah was in the cistern, he knew that he would die quickly if not rescued. Although the cistern was without water, it was swampy with mud and Jeremiah was sinking into it. He must die soon, if not by suffocation, by exposure.

Ebedmelech went to the king and confronted him with the injustice that he had permitted. He got authority to carry out a rescue operation. He took three men with him, got ropes, went to the palace wardrobe and got rags, and then went to the cistern. He lowered the ropes to Jeremiah and instructed him to put the rags under his armpits so that the ropes would not cut into his flesh as they pulled him out. He rescued Jeremiah.

Jeremiah was never popular. He was never surrounded with applause. But he was not friendless. In fact, Jeremiah was extremely fortunate in his friends. Twenty years or so earlier, under King Jehoiakim, Jeremiah was almost murdered, but Ahikam ben Shaphan intervened and saved him (Jer 26:24). Baruch was his disciple and secretary, loyal and faithful, sticking with him through difficult times to the very end. And Ebedmelech, the Ethiopian eunuch, came to his aid. "One friend in a lifetime is much," wrote Henry Adams, "two are many; three are hardly possible."[7] Jeremiah had three.

Ebedmelech risked his life in rescuing Jeremiah. Being a foreigner he had no legal rights. He was going against popular opinion in a crisis that was hysterical with wartime emotion. That didn't matter. A friend is a friend. Ebedmelech didn't indulge in sentimental pity for Jeremiah, philosophically lamenting his fate; he went to the king, he got ropes, he even thought of getting rags for padding so that the ropes would not cut, he enlisted help, and he pulled him out of the cistern. He acted out his friendship.

Not everyone in Jerusalem that year was just doing his job. Not all were sailing under the winds of popular opinion. There were a few people for whom a friend was more significant than a job, for whom a friend was more significant than a calculated advantage, for whom a friend meant a commitment and was worth a risk.

The simple fact that he had friends says something essential about Jeremiah: he *needed* friends. He was well-developed in his interior life. It was impossible to deter him from his course by enmity or by flattery. He was habituated to solitude. But he needed friends. No one who is whole is self-sufficient. The whole life, the complete life, cannot be lived with haughty independence. Our goal cannot be to not need anyone. One of the evidences of Jeremiah's wholeness was his capacity to receive friendship, to let others help him, to be accessible to mercy. It is easier to extend friendship to others than to receive it ourselves. In giving friendship we share strength, but in receiving it we show weakness. But well-developed persons are never garrisoned behind dogmas or projects, but rather they are alive to a wide spectrum of relationships.

The theological ideas, historical forces and righteous causes that touched Jeremiah's life never remained or became abstract but were worked out with persons, persons with names. He never used labels that lumped people into depersonalized categories. It can come as no surprise to find that there are more personal names in the book of Jeremiah than in any other prophetic book.[8]

14 I Bought the Field at Anathoth

*And I bought the field at Anathoth from Hanamel my cousin,
and weighed out the money to him, seventeen shekels of silver.
I signed the deed, sealed it, got witnesses, and weighed the
money on scales. . . . For thus says the LORD of hosts, the God
of Israel: Houses and fields and vineyards shall again be
bought in this land.*

*After I had given the deed of purchase to Baruch the son
of Neriah, I prayed to the LORD, saying: "Ah Lord GOD!
It is thou who hast made the heavens and the earth by thy great
power and by thy outstretched arm! Nothing is too hard for
thee. . . . Behold, the siege mounds have come up to the city to
take it, and because of sword and famine and pestilence the
city is given into the hands of the Chaldeans who are fighting
against it. What thou didst speak has come to pass, and
behold, thou seest it. Yet thou, O Lord GOD, hast said to me,
'Buy the field for money and get witnesses'—though the city is
given into the hands of the Chaldeans."*

*The word of the LORD came to Jeremiah: "Behold, I am the
LORD, the God of all flesh; is anything too hard for me? . . .*

*"Just as I have brought all this great evil upon this people,
so I will bring upon them all the good that I promise them.
Fields shall be bought in this land of which you are saying, It is
a desolation, without man or beast; it is given into the hands
of the Chaldeans. Fields shall be bought for money, and
deeds shall be signed and sealed and witnessed."*

Jeremiah 32:9-10, 15-17, 24-27, 42-44

I can stick artificial flowers on this tree that will not flower; or I can create the conditions in which the tree is likely to flower naturally. I may have to wait longer for my real flowers; but they are the only true ones.

John Fowles[1]

The word *practical* has been lifted from run-of-the-mill discourse and set apart as a virtue. To describe a person as practical is to give high praise. To name a person as impractical is to dismiss as irrelevant. Antique virtues, like justice and fortitude, love and faith, maintain a precarious half-life in obscurity while the parvenu virtue, practicality, preens itself at the apex of our values.

Americans have contributed in special ways to the honor of this adjective. The hallmark of America is the practical. Americans have made their mark in the world with their single-minded practicality. We are quick; we don't waste time. We are efficient; we don't waste energy. We are down-to-earth; we don't get taken in by harebrained schemes. We get things done. We make things happen. And if as individuals we don't act up to these high standards, we extravagantly admire those who do. We lead the world in knowing how to get things done.[2]

Biblical and Practical

I applaud the emphasis. This claim to be practical is a basic stance of biblical faith. It can be fairly stated, in fact, that *biblical* and *practical* are essentially synonymous. If it is practical, it is biblical; if it is biblical, it is practical. Biblical faith rejects, fiercely and unhesitatingly, any conduct or thinking that diminishes our ability to function as human beings in time and space. Ideas that drive a wedge between God and creation are false. Prayers or acts of devotion that divert or incapacitate us from the here and now are spurious. Biblical faith everywhere and always warns against siren voices that lead people away from specific and everyday engagement with weather and politics, dogs and neighbors, shopping lists and job assignments. No true spiritual life can be distilled from or abstracted out of this world of chemicals and molecules, paying your bills and taking out the garbage.[3]

But if I applaud the emphasis on the practical and find it deeply biblical, I find myself in frequent disagreement with what is supposed to be practical. We have great enthusiasm for the practical in our society, but much confusion and no little bit of ignorance surround what is in fact practical. In the confusion and ignorance great crowds of people live extremely impractical lives and engage in hopelessly impractical acts, all the while supposing themselves to be hardheaded, no-nonsense, practical people.

Jeremiah's Practicality
Jeremiah was one of the most practical persons who ever lived. All his ideas and beliefs got turned into actions, and his actions were so on target that the history of his century was in large measure the lengthened shadow of his personal history. One of the most practical things that he did was to buy a field for seventeen dollars. At the time he did it he was judged an impractical fool. People watching him buy that field thought that he was buying the Brooklyn Bridge.

Jeremiah's sense of the practical conflicted constantly with the impracticality of the people around him. Jeremiah was convinced that he lived in a creation that was made to work and work well—a *practical* creation. Everything mattered and what happened to everything—to people, to mountains, to flowers, whatever—mattered. It is an affront to God when things don't work, when people live badly. It is scandalous to substitute sham posturing in a place of worship for devout love and faith with God. Gaping wounds are opened in the body of creation when the poor and unfortunate, God's creatures every one, are cruelly exploited.

Jeremiah's sense of the practical was built on the belief

that God is the most important reality with which he and
the people with whom he lived had to deal. He said that in-
sistently and persuasively all his life. He believed that every
person is made for a relationship with God, and without
that relationship acknowledged and nurtured we live falsely and therefore impractically. People try to be good without God and it doesn't work. We try to live the good life
and not the God life, and it doesn't work. The waste of our
underdimensioned lives is appalling, and Jeremiah was
appalled. It is impossible to live thus without unfortunate
consequences. Jeremiah pleaded: "A voice on the bare
heights is heard, the weeping and pleading of Israel's sons,
because they have perverted their way, they have forgotten
the LORD their God. 'Return, O faithless sons, I will heal
your faithlessness' " (Jer 3:21-22). Reality won't put up with
unreality. Nature, including human nature, warned Cov-
entry Patmore, "will not bear any absolute and sustained
contradiction. She must be converted, not outraged."[4]

The pleadings were ignored and the judgment came.
Babylonian armies captured the city and took the leaders of
the people into exile. Eleven years (598 to 587 B.C.) followed in which the people who were left behind had a measure of personal freedom but were politically subject to
Babylon. They could have continued decent lives in those
conditions, but after several years of restlessness and agita-
tion they plotted to throw off the Babylonian yoke by enlisting Egypt in an alliance. It didn't work. The conspiracy
provoked a severe Babylonian reprisal. The Egyptians saw
that they could get no profit out of the affair and abandoned the scene. Judah was hopelessly outclassed militarily
by the Babylonians. It was the blackest time in their history. Doomsday was just around the corner. In a matter of
weeks, maybe only days, the city would be plundered and
everyone marched off to exile. There was absolutely no
hope at all.

Jeremiah, during these weeks, was shut up in prison. He had been accused of collaboration with the enemy, a false charge, but in the war hysteria it stuck. He was an unpopular figure at best, and so, as far as the people were concerned, prison was not an inappropriate place for him. In this prison—we must imagine a kind of loose confinement in the palace court where he was openly visible and had access to visitors—Jeremiah did what at the time appeared absolutely crazy: he bought a field for seventeen dollars.

It was crazy because at the very moment that he was buying it, the Babylonian armies were camping on it. He himself was in prison with no prospects for getting out. The enemy was pounding the city walls and about to take the people off to exile. At that moment Jeremiah bought a field on which he would never plant an olive tree, prune a grapevine, or build a house—a field that in all probability he would never even see.

Why did he do it? For the most practical of reasons: he did it because he was convinced that the troubles everyone was experiencing were at that very moment being used by God in what would eventually turn out to be the salvation of that land. The essential reality for Jeremiah was not that the Babylonians were camped on that field in Anathoth (although there was no denial of that fact) but that God was using that ground to fulfill his promises. He bought the field as an investment in God's next project for Israel, an investment that, as we now know, paid off admirably. "As long as matters are really hopeful," wrote Chesterton, "hope is mere flattery or platitude. It is only when everything is hopeless that hope begins to be a strength at all. Like all the Christian virtues, it is as unreasonable as it is indispensable."[5]

Jeremiah had preached God's judgment for years. Now that the judgment is at hand he alertly directs attention to the purpose of the judgment, which is to prepare lives to receive the promise of salvation. He does not say, "I told you so." He does not smugly survey the unavoidable evidence that he had been right. He is not interested in building a reputation as an accurate forecaster. He is not interested in checking off a list of fulfilled predictions. He is a practical man, interested in how the purposes of God can fill the present, changing it from futility that envelops the city like fog to hope. He takes no time out to enjoy the discomfiture of his detractors. It is God and persons with whom he has to do.

So at the moment that judgment is at hand he speaks the word that evokes hope. There is more here than Babylonians at the gate; there is God in your midst. Judgment is here. But don't despair; it is God's judgment. Face it. Accept the suffering. Experience the chastening action. God is not against you; he is for you. God has not rejected you; he is working with you. "It is a time of distress for Jacob; yet he shall be saved out of it" (Jer 30:7). "Why do you cry out over your hurt? . . . For I will restore health to you, and your wounds I will heal, says the LORD" (Jer 30:15, 17).

Judgment is not the last word; it is never the last word. Judgment is necessary because of centuries of hardheartedness; its proper work is to open our hearts to the reality beyond ourselves, to crack the carapace of self-sufficiency so that we can experience the inrushing grace of the healing, merciful, forgiving God.

> *The people who survived the sword*
> *found grace in the wilderness. . . .*
> *I have loved you with an everlasting love;*
> *therefore I have continued my faithfulness to you.*
> *Again I will build you, and you shall be built,*
> *O virgin Israel!*
> *Again you shall adorn yourself with timbrels,*
> *and shall go forth in the dance of the merrymakers. (Jer 31:2-4)*

This is not the cold language of the courtroom, nor is it the

angry language of reprisal and revenge. It is the personal
pathos of a parent.

> *Is Ephraim my dear son?*
>   *Is he my darling child?*
> *For as often as I speak against him,*
>   *I do remember him still.*
> *Therefore my heart yearns for him;*
>   *I will surely have mercy on him, says the LORD. (Jer 31:20)*

When the people were prosperous, they supposed that
nothing could interrupt or interfere with their self-satisfied
careers. During those years Jeremiah preached judgment.
Now that calamity is all around them they believe that
nothing can make things better. While the Babylonian siege
engines are pounding the walls and hourly reports on the
encroaching Babylonian devastators are posted, Jeremiah
from his prison in the palace court (a distinctly unhopeful
place) pours out his message: "There is hope for your
future, says the LORD" (Jer 31:17).

But the message of hope is no more believed than the
message of judgment had been, and for the same reason.
Anything that isn't corroborated by daily press releases and
news bulletins is dismissed as impractical.

The Field at Anathoth

One day while all this was going on, Jeremiah's cousin Hanamel came into the courtyard where Jeremiah was confined
and offered to sell him a plot of ground out in Anathoth,
Jeremiah's hometown, three miles northeast of Jerusalem.
Was Hanamel serious? Was he mocking Jeremiah? Babylonian armies were camped all over Anathoth. It was as if
someone told me that he believed that in our lifetime people on earth would inhabit Mars and I said, "Terrific. Let
me sell you an acre of land right on the main canal." Or as if
someone assured me of her confidence that before long
there would be a stable, lasting peace in the Middle East,

and I jumped in with an offer to sell her a franchise in Iranian oil wells.

Jeremiah had been saying, "Keep your voice from weeping, and your eyes from tears. . . . There is hope for your future, says the LORD, and your children shall come back to their own country" (Jer 31:16-17). Immediately Hanamel stepped up and said, "Buy my field which is at Anathoth in the land of Benjamin, for the right of possession and redemption is yours; buy it for yourself" (Jer 32:8).

What would a practical person do with such an offer? I imagine Jeremiah shuffling and temporizing: "You don't quite understand, Hanamel, I'm speaking in symbols and metaphors. I'm talking of your interior life, the way our unconscious is in touch with God's purpose. Don't be such a literalist. And don't try to unload that worthless piece of property in Anathoth on me. Just because I am a preacher doesn't mean that I'm stupid. I know the value of a buck just as well as the next man." Saying that, all the bystanders would have cheered—maybe Jeremiah wasn't such a goose as they had thought.

But that is not what happened. What is reported is that Jeremiah, deeply in touch with a reality that most of us ignore and without anxiety about what people thought about him, promptly bought the field. He weighed out seventeen shekels of silver, got the required witnesses, signed and sealed the deeds. He then instructed his friend Baruch to put the official deeds in a pottery jar to preserve them "that they may last for a long time. For thus says the LORD of hosts, the God of Israel: Houses and fields and vineyards shall again be bought in this land" (Jer 32:14-15).

Jeremiah knew that buying that field looked impractical and foolish. It was against history, against reason, against public opinion. But he didn't buy the field on the advice of his broker, but by the leading of God. He was not planning a retirement cabin on the property; he was witnessing an involvement in the continuity of God's promises. All the same, he couldn't have helped *feeling* foolish—and so he prayed, recentering himself in God's word: "Ah Lord GOD! It is thou who has made the heavens and the earth by thy great power and by thy outstretched arm! Nothing is too hard for thee. ... Behold, the siege mounds have come up to the city to take it, and because of sword and famine and pestilence the city is given into the hands of the Chaldeans who are fighting against it. ... Yet thou, O Lord GOD, hast said to me, 'Buy the field for money and get witnesses'—though the city is given into the hands of the Chaldeans" (Jer 32:17, 24-25).

As he prays the confirmation is provided: "Behold, I am the LORD, the God of all flesh; is anything too hard for me? ... Just as I have brought all this great evil upon this people, so I will bring upon them all the good that I promise them. Fields shall be bought in this land" (Jer 32:27, 42-43).

Living in Hope
Buying that field in Anathoth was a deliberate act of hope. All acts of hope expose themselves to ridicule because they seem impractical, failing to conform to visible reality. But in fact they are the reality that is being constructed but is not yet visible. Hope commits us to actions that connect with God's promises.

What we call hoping is often only wishing. We want things we think are impossible, but we have better sense than to spend any money or commit our lives to them. Biblical hope, though, is an act—like buying a field in Anathoth. Hope acts on the conviction that God will complete the work that he has begun even when the appearances, especially when the appearances, oppose it.

William Stringfellow, who has extensive personal experience with "Babylon," agrees with Jeremiah: "Hope is reliance upon grace in the face of death: the issue is that of receiving life as a gift, not as a reward and not as a punishment; hope is living constantly, patiently, expectantly, resiliently, joyously in the efficacy of the word of God."[6] Every person we meet must be drawn into that expectation. Every situation in which we find ourselves must be included in the kingdom that we are convinced God is bringing into being. Hope is buying into what we believe. We don't turn away in despair. We don't throw up our hands in disgust. We don't write this person off as incorrigible. We don't withdraw from a complex world that is too much for us.

It is, of course, far easier to languish in despair than to live in hope, for when we live in despair we don't have to do anything or risk anything. We can live lazily and shiftlessly with an untarnished reputation for practicality, current with the way things appear. It is fashionable to espouse the latest cynicism. If we live in hope, we go against the stream.

Getting Practical

I find it bordering on the incomprehensible when someone says, "Well, the Bible is all well and good in its place, but after all, when it comes down to the nitty-gritty, we have to get practical, don't we? Jeremiah, after all, never had to meet a payroll." People like that remind me of George Eliot's Mr. Tulliver, who "considered that church was one thing and common sense another, and he wanted nobody to tell *him* what common sense was."[7]

But the great looming fact is this: In the flurry and panic of that day in Jerusalem, not at all unlike any randomly selected day in anyone's week, with the populace divided between a dull acquiescence to the inevitable and wild schemes for escape, the single practical act that stands out from the historical record is that Jeremiah bought a field in Anathoth for seventeen shekels. That act made the word of God visible, made a foothold of it for anyone who wanted to make a way out of chaotic despair into the ordered wholeness of salvation. Many made their way out.

We have to get practical. Really practical. The most practical thing we can do is hear what God says and act in appropriate response to it. "Arguments are ineffectual unless supported by events."[8] Hope-determined actions participate in the future that God is bringing into being. These acts are rarely spectacular. Usually they take place outside sacred settings. Almost never are they perceived to be significant by bystanders. It is not easy to act in hope because most of the immediate evidence is against it. As a result, we live in one of the most impractical societies the world has ever seen. If we are to live practically, we must frequently defy the impracticalities of our peers. It takes courage to act in hope. But it is the only practical action, for it is the only action that survives the decay of the moment and escapes the scrapheap of yesterday's fashion.

15 Concerning the Nations

The word of the LORD *which came to Jeremiah the prophet concerning the nations. About Egypt . . . concerning the Philistines . . . concerning Moab . . . concerning the Ammonites . . . concerning Edom . . . concerning Damascus . . . concerning Kedar and the kingdoms of Hazor . . . concerning Elam . . . concerning Babylon . . .*

Jeremiah 46:1-2; 47:1; 48:1; 49:1, 7, 23, 28, 34; 50:1

Were the Gentiles to be abandoned to their own myth and to their own fate and regarded from the viewpoint of their own religion, they would constitute no part of God's creation; they would stand outside, a total negation. That however is not, and never has been the case. They are not abandoned to their myth or their fate, but are involved from the outset in God's mighty acts of creation; they belong to the earth which the Lord has rescued out of the primeval ocean; they are "the ends" towards which God's purpose is directed, the ultimate reason for the work which he has begun on his mountain of Zion, centre of the earth.

Arend Th. Van Leeuwen[1]

I grew up in a small Western town, an out-of-the-way place that was of no consequence to anyone other than the people who lived there. No one in my family or among my acquaintances traveled. We were isolated and out of touch with great events and important people. The exceptions were peripheral. I had an uncle, for instance, who had served in the infantry in World War I and had been wounded in France. I heard his war stories. Several of my maternal uncles and aunts had come from Norway when they were young, and there were stories of the farms and fjords that gave color to holiday gatherings. My paternal grandfather carried the accents of Sweden in his daily speech, but he never talked about the land of his birth. That was about it. It was not a propitious place in which to acquire a realistic conception of the world's size and complexity.

Yet by the time I was ten years old I had a lively acquaintance with the great diversity of languages and customs, climate and terrain that the earth comprises. I didn't acquire this through school studies, although I am sure that attempts were made there to give it to me. I got it in church. There were frequent visitors from remote corners of the world who came to our church. Often they were given a place to sleep in our home. Conversation at our breakfast table included references to the elephants of Africa and the temples of India, the lakes of Finland and the jungles of Brazil, the dances in Indonesia and the songs of the Congo. These people carried artifacts with them and photographs. They overflowed with stories. My childhood memories are vivid with the impressions that these missionaries made on me with their stories and zest, their passion and their prayers. I did not so much grow up in a small town as in a global village.

Among Christians my experience is typical. For biblical religion is aggressively internationalist. People who participate in the community of faith find themselves in a company of men and women who have a passion for crossing boundaries—linguistic, racial, geographic, cultural—in order to demonstrate that there is no spot on earth and no person on earth that is not included in the divine plan.

A Global Village

This quality is not recent, it is original. It has nothing to do with the human curiosity to explore or the technology of the scientific age. It is rooted in the nature of God and the reality of faith. The missionary, not the media, gave us the global village. At the time of his call Jeremiah was designated "prophet to the nations" (Jer 1:5). The word *nations (goyim)* specifically refers to the nations across the border, the others, the foreigners. He was not appointed as prophet to the Hebrews nor installed as chaplain to the court of Judah.

The title "prophet to the nations" is a deliberate rejection of any understanding of the life of faith that is identified with a single nation or a particular culture. The human task is to grow in conscious and healthy relationship with all reality, and God is the largest part of reality. If God is understood as being local, a tribal deity, he is misunderstood, and our lives are correspondingly reduced. Jeremiah battled against small-minded religion all his life. He attacked every tendency to make the temple into a cozy place. He worked strenuously and imaginatively to show the people that they were not the only people that God had dealings with, and that the life of faith necessarily involves us in a worldwide community that includes strange-appearing, strange-acting and strange-sounding people.

Biblical faith always has and always will have this global dimension to it. The promise to Abraham was that in him "all the families of the earth shall bless themselves" (Gen 12:3). D. T. Niles documents the biblical base: "The God who chose Israel out of the nations and gave it a distinctive history remained also and always the God of the nations too. The same God who brought Israel from Egypt, brought the Philistines from Caphtor and the Syrians from Kir (Amos 9:7). He is concerned with the life of the nations for He is their God (Jer. 20:4; Is. 10:5)."[2] The final vision of the Apocalypse shows the nations walking in the light of God's glory and eating of the tree of life (Rev 21:24; 22:2). God is not geographically restricted to Palestine; his mercy extends to the far corners of the earth. Jeremiah is named prophet to the nations because the God he proclaims is God of the nations. Since God is not confined in the local, the life of faith cannot be restricted to the local.

Religions that we make up for ourselves always reduce reality to what we feel comfortable with, or what makes us comfortable. We love being insiders. We feel secure when we are with cronies who talk our language and sing our songs and don't rock the boat. It hardly matters that such a life is banal, it is *safe*. "Why does man accept to live a trivial life?" asks Ernest Becker. His answer: "Because of the danger of a full horizon of experience, of course."[3] The danger is not to our humanity, but to our sense of running life on our own terms, managing people and things with ourselves at the center. The larger the world, the less of it we can subject to our own control. But that is a miserable ambition and a certain prescription for boredom. It is God's world and God rules it. Our wholeness comes from participating in what God is doing, not manipulating what we can manage. So the Bible continually protests all forms of isolationism. The great missionary statesman John R. Mott said, "The missionary activities of the church are the circulation of its blood, which would lose its vital power if it never flowed to the extremities."[4]

Prophet to the Nations

But Jeremiah never left Jerusalem and its immediate en-
virons.[5] At the end of his life he was taken against his will to
Egypt, but that hardly justifies the title "prophet to the nations." How did Jeremiah carry out his appointment to the
nations without ever leaving Jerusalem? He did it by com-
posing oracles for ten different nations: Egypt, Philistia,
Moab, Ammon, Edom, Damascus, Kedar, Hazor, Elam and
Babylon. The geographical range represented by these nations is immense, from Egypt in the west to Elam in the east,
a distance of about 1500 miles, and from Damascus in the
north to Edom in the south, a distance of 500 miles—
750,000 square miles. He may never have left Jerusalem, but
he was mentally and spiritually a world traveler. These oracles are collected in chapters 46-51 in the book of Jeremiah.

With a single exception we do not know how these messages were delivered. The exception is the message to Babylon. Jeremiah enlisted Seriah to take it with him on an
official diplomatic journey and commissioned him to read
it to the Babylonians. He also instructed him in its dramatic
disposition. When he had completed reading it, Seriah was
to take a stone and tie it to the scroll, throw it into the middle
of the River Euphrates that flowed alongside Babylon and
announce: "Thus shall Babylon sink, to rise no more, because of the evil that I am bringing upon her" (Jer 51:64).
The *way* the message was delivered was as important as
that it was delivered.

For the other nations we have no information. Would
those messages have been delivered similarly, by getting a
traveling merchant or soldier or government official to take
it? The conjecture is by no means implausible. But if we
don't know how they were delivered, we do know that the
messages were carefully and accurately prepared.

Jeremiah's messages to the ten nations were prepared
with the same seriousness as the messages that he delivered

personally in Jerusalem. Jeremiah preached with great power and poetic craft. He never spoke in clichés or slogans. He treated language with immense respect. Words had a holy quality; they were precious gifts treated with reverence and care. Marianne Moore wrote of the need for humility, concentration and gusto in the use of words. Humility she describes as the necessary armor. By concentration she means the intensity that makes for clear language; for her, gusto is the spontaneity which humility and skill make possible.[6] These qualities are evident in everything we have from Jeremiah. The messages to the nations exhibit the same exuberant yet controlled strength. John Bright values these messages as "some of the finest poetry in the entire prophetic canon."[7] They are not second-level works tossed off in a slovenly manner because they are for despised foreigners.

Jeremiah took as much care in proclaiming God's word to people he would never see as he did in addressing the people he grew up with and lived with. An examination of the messages shows that he cared enough about the ten nations to acquire thorough and detailed knowledge about them. We expect Jeremiah to take *God* seriously and to speak God's word with care, but it is a surprise to find that he has painstakingly studied these *peoples* that mean nothing to him personally. All of these oracles show an extraordinary knowledge of the geography, the history and the politics of these nations. He was not interested in them in general but in particular. He bothered to find out the details of their lives. He spoke God's word in relation to the actual conditions of their existence. This feature makes our understanding of the messages more difficult, for many of the geographical features and political allusions can no longer be determined. But every difficulty we encounter in reading the text represents a local detail in which the Philistine and the Babylonian recognized that they were being addressed with attentive and personal seriousness. The nations were not lumped together as "pagans" or "lost sinners" and then assaulted with stereotyped formulas.

I once knew a man who had come to this country after World War II as a displaced person. He had been a skilled cabinetmaker in his home country but after the war had to settle for a job as sexton in a church. Not long after I became a pastor in that same church I also became a father. Toys began to accumulate around the house. Knowing of his dexterity with tools and lumber, I asked Gus if he would throw together a toy box for me when he had a few minutes. I wanted a storage bin for the toys; I knew Gus could do it in an hour or so. Weeks later he presented our family with a carefully designed and skillfully crafted toy box. My casual request had not been treated casually. All I had wanted was a box; what I got was a piece of furniture. I was pleased, but also embarrassed. I was embarrassed because what I thought would be done in an off hour had taken many hours of work. I expressed my embarrassment. I laced my gratitude with apologies. His wife reproached me: "But you must understand that Gus is a cabinetmaker. He could never, as you say, 'throw' a box together. His pride would not permit it." That toy box has been in our family for over twenty years now and rebukes me whenever I am tempted to do hasty or shoddy work of any kind.

In a similar way Jeremiah was a prophet. It didn't matter who he was speaking to, whether they were essential to his everyday life or a passing acquaintance, people he would live with for his entire life or someone he would never see: he was a prophet. He couldn't "throw" an oracle together, "toss off" a sermon. His commitment would not permit it. He took the ten nations, although they were a minor part of his everyday ministry, as seriously as he took his own nation.

Warning and Judgment

The content of the messages that Jeremiah preached to the nations was virtually the same as that preached to his own people: warning and judgment that anticipates salvation. Egypt is promised judgment: "Prepare yourselves baggage for exile, O inhabitants of Egypt! For Memphis shall become a waste, a ruin, without inhabitant" (Jer 46:19). She is also promised salvation: "Afterward Egypt shall be inhabited as in the days of old, says the LORD" (Jer 46:26).

Moab is lamented and mourned: "The calamity of Moab is near at hand and his affliction hastens apace. Bemoan him, all you who are round about him, and all who know his name; say, 'How the mighty scepter is broken, the glorious staff' " (Jer 48:16-17). But the last word is "Yet I will restore the fortunes of Moab in the latter days, says the LORD" (Jer 48:47).

The Ammonites are addressed: "Gird yourselves with sackcloth, lament, and run to and fro among the hedges! For Milcom [their god] shall go into exile, with his priests and his princes" (Jer 49:3). Still, the final word is "But afterward I will restore the fortunes of the Ammonites, says the LORD" (Jer 49:6).

Elam is warned: "I will break the bow of Elam, the mainstay of their might; and I will bring upon Elam the four winds from the four quarters of heaven; and I will scatter them to all those winds" (Jer 49:35-36). But the characteristic last word is "But in the latter days I will restore the fortunes of Elam, says the LORD" (Jer 49:39).

The bulk of the material is devoted to judgment. The anticipation of salvation is, in each instance, a single line. But those spare lines prevent the messages from being understood as the vengeful anger of an outsider crying doom. The intimations of hope are not explicit in all the messages, but neither are they always expressed in messages to Israel. The fact that they are there at all shows that judgment is in the service of salvation, the salvation of the nations as well as of Israel. There is not one message for the insider and another for the outsider. The biblical message is the same for Jew and Gentile. As Paul puts it, "Are we Jews any better off? No, not at all; for I have already charged that all men, both Jews and Greeks, are under the power of sin" (Rom 3:9).

Concerning the Nations

Jeremiah wrote concerning the nations: specifically named, attentively described, seriously addressed. What anthropologists call ethnocentricity—the unthinking assumption that one's own people are the best while other people, especially those who constitute a threat, are considered inferior—he clearly rejected. Kenneth Cragg, reflecting on this reality and meditating on its implications through the centuries of faith experience, wrote: "The Gospel as such has no native country. He who goes out humbly with Christ in the world of all races will perpetually discover the multiple, but constant, relevance of what he takes. It takes a whole world to understand a whole Christ. . . . Those who take are not vulgarly universalizing their own culture: they are conveying that by the apprehension of which both they and their hearers learn. If the claims of the Gospel are valid it could not be otherwise."[8]

Reaching out is an act of wholeness, not only for others but for us: "It takes a whole world to understand a whole Christ." Crossing the boundaries and exploring the horizons (whether imaginatively like Jeremiah or bodily like Seriah) demonstrates God's universal love, but it also develops our own deepest health. For we cannot be whole enclosed in our own habits, even if they are pious habits. We cannot grow to maturity confined within our own coterie, even if it is a very orthodox coterie. We cannot grow an oak tree in a barrel; it needs acres of earth under it and oceans of sky above it. Neither can we grow a human being in a narrow sect, a ghettoized religion. The larger the world we live in, the larger our lives develop in response. At least one of the reasons for Jeremiah's heroic stature is his concern for the Elamites. We cannot be whole human beings if we cut ourselves off from the environment which God created and in which he is working. People of faith live in a far larger reality than people without faith. "God so loved the *world*."

We often betray this reality. We huddle and retreat. We ignore and even despise outsiders. We collect a few friends who look alike and think alike. We reject any suggestion that we transcend biological comforts and psychological securities. We barricade ourselves from visions that expose our prejudices, from people that challenge our narcissism.

André and Pierre-Emmanuel Lacocque, in a brilliant weaving of biblical, theological and psychological material, have called this the "Jonah complex"—the clash between what I feel good about in myself and what I am under commission to do for God, the tension between coziness and character.[9] Jonah was torn between his desire for an undisturbed enjoyment of his personal potential and accumulated possessions, and the fulfillment of a vocation that smashed his preconceptions and interrupted his comfortable pursuit of happiness.

Meanwhile there is Jeremiah, and the people like him who keep showing up in our homes and communities and churches, who go beyond the boundaries of what is safe and comfortable, learn new languages, discover alien cultures, brave hostility and misunderstanding, and who have the scars and tell the stories that prove that the life of faith can be lived in every place and among all peoples—*must* be lived in every place, among all peoples.

16 In the Land of Egypt They Shall Fall

Hear the word of the LORD, O remnant of Judah. Thus says the LORD of hosts, the God of Israel: If you set your faces to enter Egypt and go to live there, then the sword which you fear shall overtake you there in the land of Egypt; and the famine of which you are afraid shall follow hard after you to Egypt; and there you shall die.

So Johanan the son of Kareah and all the commanders of the forces and all the people did not obey the voice of the LORD, to remain in the land of Judah. But Johanan the son of Kareah and all the commanders of the forces took all the remnant of Judah who had returned to live in the land of Judah from all the nations to which they had been driven—the men, the women, the children, the princesses, and every person whom Nebuzaradan the captain of the guard had left with Gedaliah the son of Ahikam, son of Shaphan; also Jeremiah the prophet and Baruch the son of Neriah. And they came into the land of Egypt, for they did not obey the voice of the LORD.

Therefore thus says the LORD of hosts, the God of Israel: Behold, I will set my face against you for evil, to cut off all Judah. I will take the remnant of Judah who have set their faces to come to the land of Egypt to live, and they shall all be consumed; in the land of Egypt they shall fall.

Jeremiah 42:15-16; 43:4-7; 44:11-12

Nothing could be farther from the truth than the facile belief that God only manifests Himself in progress, in the improvement of standards of living, in the spread of medicine and the reform of abuses, in the diffusion of organized Christianity. The reaction from this type of theistic meliorism, which a few years ago had almost completely supplanted the faith of Moses, and Elijah, and Jesus among modern Christians, both Protestant and Catholic, is now sweeping multitudes from their religious moorings. Real spiritual progress can only be achieved through catastrophe and suffering, reaching new levels after the profound catharsis which accompanies major upheavals. Every such period of mental and physical agony, while the old is being swept away and the new is still unborn, yields different social patterns and deeper spiritual insights.

William Foxwell Albright[1]

Every once in a while, when I get tired of living by faith, I drive twenty-five miles southwest to Memorial Stadium in Baltimore and watch the Orioles play baseball. For a couple of hours I am in a world that is defined by exactly measured lines and precise, geometric patterns. Every motion on the playing field is graceful and poised. Sloppy behavior is not tolerated. Complex physical feats are carried out with immense skill. Errors are instantly detected and their consequences immediately experienced. Rule infractions are punished directly. Unruly conduct is banished. The person who refuses to play by the rules is ejected. Outstanding performance is recognized and applauded on the spot. While the game is being played, people of widely divergent temperaments, moral values, religious commitments, and cultural backgrounds agree on a goal and the means for pursuing it. When the game is over, everyone knows who won and who lost. It is a world from which all uncertainty is banished, a world in which everything is clear and obvious. Afterward the entire experience is summarized in the starkly unambiguous vocabulary of numbers, exact to the third decimal point.

The world to which I return when the game is over contains all the elements that were visible in the stadium—elegance and sloppiness, grace and unruliness, victory and defeat, diversity and unity, reward and punishment, boundary and risk, indolence and excellence—but with a significant difference: instead of being sharply distinguished they are hopelessly muddled. What is going on at any particular time is almost never exactly clear. None of the lines are precise. The boundaries are not clear. Goals are not agreed upon. Means are in constant dispute. When I leave the world of brightly lighted geometric patterns,

I pick my way through inkblots, trying to discern the significance of the shapes with all the help from Rorschach that I can get. My digital wristwatch, for all its technological accuracy, never tells me whether I am at the beginning or in the middle or near the end of an experience. At the end of the day—or the week, or the year—there is no agreement on who has won and who has lost.

The Egyptian Alternative

When the Israelites got tired of living by faith, they went 250 miles southwest to Egypt where everything was clear and precise. They took Jeremiah with them. All his life Jeremiah had preached a faith that was intensely personal; Egypt organized a religion that was impersonally bureaucratic. It is the supreme irony of Jeremiah's life that it ended in Egypt, the place that represented everything that he abhorred.

It was not the first time that Israel had done this. The Egyptian alternative to faith asserted itself over and over again. When Abraham, father of all who live by faith, got tired of living by faith he went to Egypt (Gen 12:10-20). He hoped to find security there, but instead he was plunged into deceit and compromise. Abraham's Egyptian experiment was a near disaster for the development of faith in which he was the God-selected pioneer.

At the time of the Exodus, after the Hebrews had been delivered out of Egyptian bondage and were being trained to live by faith in the desert, the pull back to Egypt was persistent. True, they had been slaves there, but at least they were secure. They knew what to expect. The pillar of the cloud was a flimsy successor to the solid, fixed pyramids.

Later, when the monarchy was at its apogee, Solomon imported Egyptian certainties into the life of faith by making a marriage alliance with the Egyptian Pharaoh's daughter (1 Kings 9:16). It must have seemed like a marvelous idea at the time—to live by faith in the Promised Land but to build up a nest egg of Egyptian security on the side. The Egyptian marriage alliance was the first of many. Solomon, once having compromised the life of faith, found himself hopelessly entangled in attempts to secure his kingdom on all sides by marrying into all the surrounding kingdoms (1 Kings 11:1-8).

And so it was not without precedent that Israel, in the enormous confusion and muddle following the fall of Jerusalem in 586 B.C., would succumb to the age-old attraction of Egypt.

There is nothing more difficult than to live spontaneously, hopefully, virtuously—by faith. And there was never a time when the external conditions were less conducive to living by faith than in those devastating and bewildering days following the Babylonian invasion. The temple, focus for worship for half a millennium, was in rubble. The ritual, rich in allusion and meaning, was wiped out. The priestly voices, who had spoken in reassuring tones for decades, were silent. Out of this traumatic dislocation Jeremiah told the people to set aside their fears and begin a new life of faith.

It was easier to go to Egypt. So they went to Egypt. In Egypt there were no uncertainties, no loose ends, no ambiguity. Every detail in this life and the next was accounted for in Egypt.

Egypt was clear geographically. The great Nile River, a line of green life across the sere desert, divided Egypt. Along the river was life; apart from the river was death. There were no mountainous mysteries, no surprising valleys, no unexpected bursts of streams. There was simply this great river flowing in measured pace, predictable in its seasonal rhythms. All life, animal and vegetable, was ordered in relation to the river.

Egypt was clear architecturally. The pyramids and temples stood out from the landscape in precise lines. The mathematical exactitude of their construction is a marvel still. Nothing was left unexpressed in those monuments looming up from the desert. The pyramids arranged and plotted the uncertainties of death. The statuary and structures of the temples resolved the ambiguities of life. Under the cloudless Egyptian sky and on the featureless Egyptian sand, quarried and carved forms structured reality with such megalomaniac arrogance that all anxiety was banished. If there were ever doubts about the significance of an enterprise, they were chased off by the bully expedient of making it bigger.

Egypt was clear theologically. The unseen was translated into the seen. All gods were made into images. Everything that might have been more than human was reduced to what was less than human: the cat, the hawk, the hyena, the bull, the ibis were the god-images of the Egyptians. Every image was stylized, and in those stylized images all wonder was eliminated. Spontaneity was unheard of. It was a religion of absolute control. All reality was rendered in the flat surface of stone, in the anonymous language of number.

Egypt was clear socially. Everyone's place was defined hierarchically. The king was at the apex and the slave-serf at the base, with all others ranged in between. The diminishment of people was compensated for by the clarity of knowing where they stood. If there was less honor, there was also less responsibility. If there was less to hope for, there was also less to have to deal with.

Egypt was the Memorial Stadium of the ancient world: clean boundaries, set rules, a clear separation between the players (the royal house) and the spectators (everyone else), all the gods in picture form so that everyone knew who was who (you can't tell the players without a program), and, above all, numbers—everything accounted for by geometry, trigonometry, arithmetic. Straight lines. Sharp angles. Statistics.

The Clarities of Faith

Not that there are no clarities in the life of faith. There are. Vast, soaring harmonies; deep, satisfying meanings; rich, textured experiences. But these clarities develop from within. They cannot be imposed from without. They cannot be hurried. It is not a matter of hurriedly arranging "dead things into a dead mosaic, but of living forces into a great equilibrium."[2] The clarities of faith are organic and personal, not mechanical and institutional. Faith *invades* the muddle; it does not eliminate it. Peace develops in the midst of chaos. Harmony is achieved slowly, quietly, unobtrusively—like the effects of salt and light. Such clarities result from a courageous commitment to God, not from controlling or being controlled by others. Such clarities come from adventuring deep into the mysteries of God's will and love, not by cautiously managing and moralizing in ways that minimize risk and guarantee self-importance.

These clarities can only be experienced in acts of faith and only recognized with the eyes of faith. Jeremiah's life was brilliantly supplied with such clarities, but they were always surrounded by hopeless disarray. Sometimes devout and sometimes despairing, Jeremiah doubted himself and God. But these internal agonies never seemed to have interfered with his vocation and his commitment. He argued with God but he did not abandon him. He was clear at the center: it was with God that he had to do. He was committed to the covenant of God. He was unwavering in his understanding of morality. He was steady in his hope in God's mercy. But just because he was sure of God did not mean that he was always sure of himself. Nor did the world around him ever become clear. The world remained a muddle—and it will.

There is a moment in this last chapter of Jeremiah's life
when it looks as if the muddle will be banished. The moment occurs in the time after the fall of Jerusalem and just
before the escape to Egypt. The environment is the blackest
it has ever been. Then this single, luminous moment in
Jeremiah's life is framed. Every detail of the life of faith
is etched clearly against the dark disorder of the sin-ruined
Jerusalem streets and the false-front neatness of the Egyptian alternative.

The city had fallen to the Babylonians as Jeremiah had
long warned that it would. All the people were rounded up
and herded into exile as Jeremiah had predicted. The lies
of the false prophets and priests were mercilessly exposed.
The integrity of Jeremiah's preaching was confirmed. Jeremiah was put into chains along with the rest. A few of the
poorest people, seen as weak and worthless, didn't even
qualify as prisoners and were left behind. The forced-
march journey across the 700 miles of hot plains to Babylon
was begun. They were five miles out of the city when the
Babylonian captain Nebuzaradan got word from his king to
stop the march and give Jeremiah the choice of whether to
go or stay.

Imagine: Jeremiah singled out from that crowd with a
personal message from the world-conquering King Nebu-
chadnezzar. In Jerusalem Jeremiah had been laughed at
in the streets, thrown into a cistern to die, taunted in the
courtyard prison, put in the stocks and ridiculed. Now, half
a day into the long hard trip into exile, the action is suddenly arrested, Jeremiah is singled out, his chains are cut off
him, and Nebuzaradan presents him with a choice. He can
go to Babylon with the promise of special treatment—no
chains, no deprivation, protective custody (so that he will
never again have to endure the abuse of his fellow citizens)
and a special allowance from the King. Or he can stay in
Jerusalem, the city he has lived in and labored for all his

life. A governor has just been appointed who has been Jeremiah's good, lifelong friend (Gedeliah, son of Shaphan). Jeremiah is welcome, if he chooses, to stay with him and be part of the tiny remnant community.

Life in Jerusalem would be starting over: in a brutal environment with the scantiest of resources, human and material, in the midst of a wrecked city with a few poor people who weren't even worth being made prisoners! Not, it would seem, a very happy prospect at age sixty-five.

Life in Babylon would be an easy retirement: honored by the Babylonian court, protected by a Babylonian bodyguard, living on a Babylonian pension. Jeremiah was ready for retirement and he deserved it. After a lifetime of ridicule and rejection, hungry for recognition, he was offered an honorary degree by the most powerful king in the world. This prophet, who was either ignored or laughed at by his own countrymen, was held in awe and respect by the Babylonians.

But Jeremiah wasn't ready for retirement. He wasn't tired of living by faith. He was used to starting over with nothing. He had been doing it for a long time. He had long since quit calculating his chances by counting his resources; his habit was to expect God's grace, "new every morning." His decision was unhesitating. He chose to stay in Jerusalem. He chose the rubble, the outcasts, the poor—the remnant out of whom he believed that God would build a people to his glory.

In judged Jerusalem it was impossible to confuse material prosperity with God's blessing. It was impossible to confuse social status with God's favor. It was impossible to confuse national pride with God's glory. It was impossible to confuse rituals of religion with God's presence. The clutter of possessions was gone; the trappings of status were gone; the pride of nation was gone; the splendor of religion was gone. And God was present. All the cultural and political and religious and social assumptions and presuppositions that interfered with the clear hearing of God's word in Jeremiah's preaching were taken away. Conditions had never been better for developing a mature community of faith. Out of the emptiness God would make a new creation.

Jeremiah's choice that day at Rama is the characteristic action of his life. He chose to be where God commanded, at the center of God's action, at the place of God's promise, in the midst of God's salvation in defiance of stereotyped conventions and popular opinions and self-aggrandizing flatteries. Jeremiah chose to live by faith. Living by faith does not mean living with applause; living by faith does not mean playing on the winning team; living by faith demands readiness to live by what cannot be seen or controlled or predicted. "If we fix our eyes," wrote Karl Barth, "upon the place where the course of the world reaches its lowest point, where its vanity is unmistakable, where its groanings are most bitter and the divine incognito most impenetrable, we shall encounter there—Jesus Christ.... The transformation of all things occurs where the riddle of human life reaches its culminating point. The hope of His glory emerges for us when nothing but the existentiality of God remains, and He becomes to us the veritable and living God. He, whom we can apprehend only as against us, stands there—for us."[3]

The abyss of obscurity and contradiction and paradox in Jeremiah's life is resolved in this moment. All the skeptical question marks that had been raised over Jeremiah throughout his life—was he a true or false prophet? was he a patriot or a traitor? was he clear-sighted or deluded? was he futile or effective?—are turned into affirmative exclamation marks. The truth of his preaching is vindicated. The integrity of his life is proved. His commitment to God's covenant is validated. Finally, a happy ending!

Not the End

Except that it is not the end. The perfectly shaped moment disintegrates into chaos. The dramatic resolution collapses into a moral muddle.

No sooner had Gedeliah been installed as governor and Jeremiah gone to work developing the life of the people of God than a terrorist outlaw, Ishmael, murdered governor Gedeliah, slaughtered everyone in the vicinity and threw their corpses into a giant cistern. A real bloodbath. His action was countered by one Johanan who rallied the survivors, chased Ishmael out of the country and set about restoring order again.

The first and best thing that Johanan did was to ask Jeremiah to pray for God's guidance. Jeremiah prayed. God gave direction consistent with Jeremiah's previous decision: the people were to stay in Jerusalem. They were to be the remnant people out of whom God would develop his holy nation. They were, in other words, to live by faith. "If you will remain in this land, then I will build you up and not pull you down; I will plant you, and not pluck you up. . . . I will grant you mercy" (Jer 42:10, 12).

Johanan and the people respected Jeremiah enough to ask for his prayers, but they didn't trust God enough to follow his counsel. They were tired of living by faith. They decided to go to Egypt. Fear was one motive. They feared Babylonian reprisal for Ishmael's terrorist assassination. But the big reason was a refusal to live by faith. They didn't want the risk and hazard of depending on an invisible God. They wanted the security and stability of a solid economy. They didn't want the hard work of rebuilding a life of faith in God. They wanted the soft life that they thought awaited them in Egypt: "No, we will go to the land of Egypt, where we shall not see war, or hear the sound of the trumpet, or be hungry for bread, and we will dwell there" (Jer 42:14). They were looking for an easy way out.

Far too many people choose to live in Egypt instead of by faith. They go to religion the way I go to a baseball game —to escape the muddle, to have everything clear, to find a good seat from which they can see the whole scene at a glance, evaluate everyone's performance easily and see people get what they deserve. Moral box scores are carefully penciled in. Statistics are obsessively kept. Many religious meetings are designed to meet just such desires. The world is reduced to what can be organized and regulated; every person is clearly labeled as being on your side or on the other side; there is never any doubt about what is good and what is bad.

The only problem with such "Egyptian" religion is that the clarity lasts only as long as the meeting. It is not a deepening of reality but a vacation from it. During that protected time and space, heroic performances are applauded and villains booed. There is a clear-cut opposition to hate. But back at work, at play, at home, the labels don't stick. Life outside the meeting is then resented as being hopelessly contaminated. It is understandable that people who embrace this kind of religious life go to as many meetings as possible in order to have the experience of clear and controlled order as frequently as possible.

Neither Shot nor Married

Flannery O'Connor once remarked that she had an aunt who thought that nothing happened in a story unless somebody got married or shot at the end of it.[4] But life seldom provides such definitive endings. As a consequence, the best stories, the stories that show us our true condition by immersing us in reality, don't provide them either. Life is ambiguous. There are loose ends. It takes maturity to live with the ambiguity and the chaos, the absurdity and the untidiness. If we refuse to live with it, we exclude something, and what we exclude may very well be the essential and dear—the hazards of faith, the mysteries of God.

Jeremiah ends inconclusively. We want to know the end, but there is no end. The last scene of Jeremiah's life shows him, as he had spent so much of his life, preaching God's word to a contemptuous people (Jer 44). We want to know that he was finally successful so that, if we live well and courageously, we also will be successful. Or we want to know that he was finally unsuccessful so that, since a life of faith and integrity doesn't pay off, we can get on with finding another means by which to live. We get neither in Jeremiah. He doesn't get married and he doesn't get shot.[5] In Egypt, the place he doesn't want to be, with people who treat him badly, he continues determinedly faithful, magnificently courageous, heartlessly rejected—a towering life terrifically lived.

Notes

Chapter 1: How Will You Compete with Horses?

[1]William McNamara, *The Human Adventure* (Garden City, N.Y.: Image Books, Doubleday, 1976), p. 9; and *Mystical Passion* (New York: Paulist Press, 1977), p. 3.

[2]Tom Howard, *Chance or Dance* (Carol Stream, Ill.: Harold Shaw Publishers, 1972), p. 104.

[3]Cleanth Brooks, *The Hidden God* (New Haven: Yale University Press, 1963), p. 4.

[4]"Maslow wrote in 1968: 'the only way we can ever know what is right for us is that it feels better subjectively than any alternative'; and again: 'what tastes good is also, in the growth sense, "better" for us.' No position has been more damaging to modern society. The terms 'feel' and 'subjectivity' as criteria for 'growth' are especially deceiving. It is simply contrary to truth that one 'grows' by choosing 'what tastes good.' In many cases the opposite is true. If the Jew Abraham Maslow were right in this, there would have been no Israel in human history." André Lacocque and Pierre-Emmanuel Lacocque, *The Jonah Complex* (Atlanta: John Knox Press, 1981), p. 106.

[5]"The book of Jeremiah does not so much teach religious truths as present a religious personality. Prophecy had already taught its truths, its last effort was to reveal itself in a life." A. B. Davidson, quoted in John Skinner, *Prophecy and Religion* (London: Cambridge University Press, 1963), p. 16.

[6]James Bentley, "Vitezslav Gardavsky, Atheist and Martyr," *The Expository Times*, June 1980, pp. 276-77.

[7]Erwin Chargaff, *Heraclitean Fire* (New York: The Rockefeller University Press, 1978), p. 122.

Chapter 2: Jeremiah
[1]Eugen Rosenstock-Huessy, *Speech and Reality* (Norwich, Vermont: Argo Books, 1970), p. 167.
[2]Eugen Rosenstock-Huessy, *I Am an Impure Thinker* (Norwich, Vermont: Argo Books, 1970), pp. 41-42.
[3]Quoted by Skinner, *Prophecy and Religion,* p. 350.
[4]Rosenstock-Huessy, *I Am an Impure Thinker,* p. 66.
[5]Thomas Merton, *The New Man* (New York: Mentor-Omega Books, 1961), p. 120.
[6]George Herbert, *The Country Parson* (New York: Paulist Press, 1981), p. 85.
[7]William Faulkner, *The Town* (New York: Random House, 1957), p. 112ff.
[8]I have paraphrased. The verbatim question and answer are: "When did you first realize that you wanted to be a poet?" "I've thought about that and sort of reversed it. My question is 'when did other people give up the idea of being a poet?' You know, when we were kids we make up things, we write, and for me the puzzle is not that some people are writing, the real question is why did the other people stop?" William Stafford, *Writing the Australian Crawl* (Ann Arbor: University of Michigan Press, 1978), p. 86.
[9]Stephen Spender, "What I expected was," in *The New Oxford Book of English Verse 1250-1950,* ed. Helen Gardner (New York: Oxford University Press, 1972), p. 930.

Chapter 3: Before
[1]Pierre Teilhard de Chardin, *The Divine Milieu* (New York: Harper and Bros., 1960), pp. 48-49.
[2]"Men are still men, and not keyboards of pianos over which the hands of Nature may play at their own sweet will." Fyodor Dostoyevsky, *Letters from the Underworld* (New York: E. P. Dutton & Co., 1957), p. 36.
[3]Quoted by E. F. Schumacher, *A Guide for the Perplexed* (New York: Perennial Library, Harper & Row, 1977), p. 6.

Chapter 4: I Am Only a Youth
[1]J. R. R. Tolkien, *The Fellowship of the Ring* (Boston: Houghton Mifflin, 1965), p. 70.
[2]Schumacher, *A Guide for the Perplexed,* p. 38.
[3]William Barrett, *Irrational Man* (Garden City, N.Y.: Doubleday Anchor Books, 1962), p. 3.
[4]W. H. Auden, "Reflections in a Forest," *Homage to Clio* (New York: Random House, 1960), p. 8.
[5]Blaise Pascal, *Pensées* (New York: The Modern Library, Random

House, 1941), p. 273.

[6]Quoted by Maisie Ward, *Gilbert Keith Chesterton* (Baltimore: Penguin Books, 1958), p. 114.

[7]That is not to say that everybody admitted it. The false prophets throughout Jeremiah's lifetime reassured the people that everything would be all right. And the kings continued to arrange political alliances to stave off disaster. But the shrillness of the positive-thinking preaching and the desperation in the treaty making betrayed the knowledge that doomsday was threatening.

Chapter 5: Do Not Trust in These Deceptive Words

[1]Thomas à Kempis, *The Imitation of Christ,* translated by Ronald Knox and Michael Oakley (New York: Sheed and Ward, 1959), pp. 76-77.

[2]Also see John Bright, *The Kingdom of God* (Nashville: Abingdon Press, 1953), p. 100.

[3]William Meredith, "Chinese Banyan" quoted in Richard Howard, *Alone with America* (New York: Atheneum, 1969), p. 324.

[4]John Bright, *A History of Israel* (Philadelphia: Westminster Press, 1959), p. 299.

[5]Ibid., p. 297.

[6]Quoted by John W. Gardner, *Self-Renewal* (New York: Harper & Row, 1963), p. 96.

Chapter 6: Go Down to the Potter's House

[1]R. P. Blackmur, *The Lion and the Honeycomb* (New York: Harcourt, Brace & World, 1955), pp. 179-80.

[2]The line is not quite as clear as I have drawn it. Kathleen Kenyon's excavations of Jericho have shown the existence of city life previous to the invention of pottery—"pre-pottery neolithic." But granted Jericho and two or three other excavated sites as exceptions, the generalization still holds. See Kathleen Kenyon, *Digging Up Jericho* (London: Ernest Benn Ltd., 1957).

[3]George Herbert, "The Bag," *The Temple* (New York: Paulist Press, 1981), p. 276.

[4]John Bright, *Jeremiah* (Garden City, N. Y.: Doubleday, 1965), p. 125.

Chapter 7: Pashhur Beat Jeremiah

[1]Malcolm Muggeridge, *A Twentieth Century Testimony* (Nashville: Thomas Nelson, 1978), p. 72.

[2]F. O. Matthiessen, *American Renaissance* (New York: Oxford University Press, 1968), p. 182.

[3]Flannery O'Connor, *The Habit of Being,* Letters edited by Sally Fitzgerald (New York: Farrar, Straus & Giroux, 1979), p. 81.

[4]I have let my imagination roam rather freely in comparing and contrasting Pashhur and Jeremiah. Some of this comes from a textual detail that suggests that Pashhur is to be seen as a parody of Jeremiah—

Pashhur the corruption of a life that Jeremiah maintains in integrity. Jeremiah was appointed as prophet to the nations ("See, I have set you this day over nations"—Jer 1:10). The verb "I have set you" is *paqad*. The noun form of that verb is *paqid*, and appointed officer. Pashhur is such an appointee, a *paqid* ("officer in the house of the LORD"— Jer 20:1). So both men live out the role of *paqid*, Jeremiah as God's prophet, Pashhur as the temple's overseer. Pashhur, in irony, is exaggerated as *chief* appointee, *paqid nagid*. By using the same root word *(pqd)* in relation to their respective appointments, and describing the clash between them as they lived out their similar vocations in such very different ways, the text invites, it seems to me, this kind of reflection.

Chapter 8: My Wound Incurable
[1]Therese of Lisieux, *Autobiography of a Saint*, trans. Ronald Knox (London: Fontana Books, Collins, 1960), p. 94.

[2]The passages are Jeremiah 8:18—9:3; 11:18-23; 12:1-6; 15:10-12, 15-21; 17:14-18; 18:18-23; 20:7-18.

[3]"We have a record of one attempt to discover the operations of sanctity which is as diverting to us as it was frustrating to the watcher. The subject under investigation was Francis de Sales, and his arrogantly curious observer was Jean Pierre Camus, Bishop of Belley. There seems to have been no planned mischief in the trick the Bishop used, but there was certainly bad taste. For what he did was drill a hole in the wall of his bedroom in the episcopal residence so that he could spy on his host when Francis thought himself alone.... And what did Camus discover? That he crept out of bed early and quietly in the mornings so as not to wake his servant. That he prayed, wrote, answered his letters, read his office, slept, and prayed again." Phyllis McGinley, *Saint-Watching* (New York: The Viking Press, 1969), pp. 17-18.

[4]Bright, *Jeremiah*, p. 110.

[5]John A. Thompson, *The Book of Jeremiah* (Grand Rapids: Eerdmans, 1980), p. 459.

[6]Ibid., p. 398.

[7]Ibid.

[8]Walter Lippmann, *A Preface to Morals* (New York: MacMillan, 1929), p. 56.

Chapter 9: Twenty-Three Years ... Persistently
[1]Baron Friedrich von Hügel, *Selected Letters 1896-1924*, edited by Bernard Holland (New York: E. P. Dutton, 1933), pp. 305 and 266.

[2]Brown, Driver, Briggs, *Hebrew and English Lexicon of the Old Testament* (Oxford: Clarendon Press, 1957), p. 1014.

[3]Ibid.

[4]John Fowles, *The Ebony Tower* (Boston: Little, Brown & Co., 1974), p. 147.

[5]G. K. Chesterton, quoted in Ward, *Gilbert Keith Chesterton,* p. 397.

[6]Garry Wills, "Hurrah for Politicians," *Harper's Magazine,* September 1975, p. 53.

Chapter 10: Take a Scroll and Write on It

[1]Abraham Heschel, *God in Search of Man* (New York: Farrar, Straus and Giroux, 1955), p. 244.

[2]Quoted by George Steiner, *Language and Silence* (New York: Atheneum, 1970), p. 67.

[3]George Adam Smith, *Jeremiah* (London: Hodder and Stoughton, 1923), p. 146.

[4]In S. R. Driver's list of the characteristic words and expressions in Deuteronomy, the best and most complete list that has been made, *love* heads the list. See *A Critical and Exegetical Commentary on Deuteronomy* (New York: Charles Scribner's Sons, 1895), pp. lxxviii-lxxxiv.

[5]André and Pierre-Emmanuel Lacocque, *The Jonah Complex,* p. 113.

[6]Charles Williams, *The Descent of the Dove* (New York: Meridian Books, 1956), p. 83.

[7]Heschel, *God in Search of Man,* p. 237.

[8]Smith, *Jeremiah,* p. 41.

[9]King Jehoiakim's antipathy to Jeremiah is understandable. Early in the king's reign Jeremiah had dressed him down for thinking that he was a king just because he spent money like a king ("Do you think you are a king because you compete in cedar?"). He compared him unfavorably with his father, Josiah, who had administered justice in the land and honored God, whereas the son was rapacious and plundering. He predicted a donkey's death for him on the city's garbage dump: "With the burial of an ass he shall be buried, dragged and cast forth beyond the gates of Jerusalem" (Jer 22:11-19). With such rebukes ringing in his ears it is no wonder that the king had forbidden Jeremiah to speak in public.

[10]R. E. C. Browne, *The Ministry of the Word* (Philadelphia: Fortress Press, 1976), p. 23.

[11]This scroll is probably chapters 1-25, the first step in the composition of the book of Jeremiah. The complete book was the result of a long and intricate process that would include Baruch's memoirs. The formation was extremely complex. A good description of the elements in the process can be found in Thompson, *The Book of Jeremiah,* pp. 56-59.

Chapter 11: House of the Rechabites

[1]Jacques Maritain, *The Peasant of the Garonne* (New York: Holt, Rinehart and Winston, 1968), p. 172.

[2]Søren Kierkegaard insisted "the crowd is untruth." He explored the significance of this assertion in all of his writings. For instance: "There is a view of life which conceives that where the crowd is, there is also the truth, and that in truth itself there is need of having the crowd

on its side. There is another view of life which conceives that wherever there is a crowd there is untruth, so that (to consider for a moment the extreme case), even if every individual, each for himself in private, were to be in possession of the truth, yet in case they were to get together in a crowd—a crowd to which any sort of *decisive* significance is attributed, a voting, noisy, audible crowd—untruth would at once be in evidence." But Kierkegaard also carefully qualifies his position: "Perhaps it may be well to note here, although it seems to me almost superfluous, that it naturally could not occur to me to object to the fact, for example, that preaching is done or that the truth is proclaimed, even though it were to an assemblage of hundreds of thousands. Not at all; but if there were an assemblage even of only ten—and if they should put the truth to the ballot, that is to say if the assemblage should be regarded as the authority, if it is the crowd which turns the scale— then there *is* untruth." *The Point of View* (London: Oxford University Press, 1939), p. 112.

3Kierkegaard, *The Point of View,* p. 131.

4When we "admire and blubber" in the presence of superior human achievement, we turn ourselves, says Kierkegaard, into spectators and connoisseurs and neatly avoid the call to live as human beings ourselves. Admiration, in other words, can be a dodge. See Søren Kierkegaard, *Concluding Unscientific Postscript* (Princeton: Princeton University Press, 1941), pp. 320-22.

5The Rechabites have usually been described as a nomadic clan that lived a disciplined, ascetic life pasturing flocks in the wilderness. Their way of life was a protest against the decadence of civilization and an idealization of the forty wilderness years when religion was austere and untainted with the fertility rites of the agricultural communities and the immoralities associated with the cities. Recent studies have shown that there is no basis in biblical fact for that identification and argue a high degree of probability that the Rechabites were a guild of craftsmen in metal. See Frank S. Frick, "The Rechabites Reconsidered," *Journal of Biblical Literature,* 90 (1971):279-87; and "Rechabites," *Interpreter's Dictionary of the Bible, Supplement* (Nashville: Abingdon Press, 1976), pp. 726-28.

6Maxim Gorky said that he did not write to entertain; he wanted to show people how "badly and boringly they lived their lives" so that they could then go on to live them well.

7William Barrett, *The Illusion of Technique* (Garden City, N.Y.: Anchor Press/Doubleday, 1978), p. 219.

Chapter 12: Letter to the Exiles
1Peter T. Forsyth, *Positive Preaching and the Modern Mind* (London: Independent Press Ltd., 1907), pp. 178-79.

2The exile took place in two stages. King Jehoiachin, the queen mother, and most leaders were deported in 598 B.C. Most of the populace was left behind under the puppet king Zedekiah. Jeremiah, one of those left behind, wrote his letter in about 594. Eleven years after the first exile, provoked by plots and insurrectionist activity, Babylon returned in 587 and destroyed the city. At that time they took virtually everyone into exile. See John Bright, *A History of Israel* (Philadelphia: Westminster Press, 1959), pp. 302-10.

[3]Exodus 2:22. The phrase entered the popular speech of our century through the science-fiction novel of Robert A. Heinlein, *Stranger in a Strange Land* (New York: Avon Books, 1961).

[4]Robertson Davies, *Rebel Angels* (New York: Viking Press, 1981), p. 326.

[5]George Eliot, *Felix Holt* (New York: The Century Co., 1911), p. 301.

[6]His actual words: "Sinners always want what is lacking to them, and souls full of God want only what they have." Quoted by Thomas Merton, *Conjectures of a Guilty Bystander* (Garden City, N.Y.: Image/Doubleday, 1968), p. 285.

[7]Walker Percy's Binx Bolling says, "The search is what anyone would undertake if he were not sunk in the everydayness of his own life. . . . To become aware of the possibility of the search is to be onto something. Not to be onto something is to be in despair." *The Moviegoer* (New York: Avon Books, 1980), p. 18.

[8]J. A. Sanders, *Interpreter's Dictionary of the Bible*, 2:188.

[9]*William Faulkner, Lion in the Garden,* Interviews edited by James B. Merriweather and Michael Millgate (New York: Random House, 1968), p. 108.

Chapter 13: Sentry . . . King . . . Eunuch

[1]Erik H. Erikson, *Identity, Youth and Crisis* (New York: W. W. Norton and Co., 1968), p. 314.

[2]R. P. Blackmur, *Henry Adams* (New York: Harcourt Brace Jovanovich, 1980), p. 3.

[3]F. H. Heinemann, *Existentialism and the Modern Predicament* (London: Adam and Charles Black, 1954), p. 67. His contemporaries had no way of knowing it, but Jeremiah was the brightest star in what scholars centuries later would see as a constellation of religious leaders strategically placed across the world. The seventh and sixth centuries B.C. were renaissance centuries in matters of the soul and God. In other parts of the world Zarathustra was beginning a new religion in Persia; Lao-tse was formulating Taoism in China; the Buddha was beginning his great reform movement in India. In Greece the philosophers Thales and Anaximander were laying the foundations of Greek philosophy. All over the world there was yearning and hunger and thirst for righteousness. Deep thinking and ardent yearning seem to characterize what we know of the centers of civilization in China, India, Persia and Greece. In Palestine it was Jeremiah.

[4]Abraham Maslow, *The Farther Reaches of Human Nature* (New York: Viking Press, 1971), p. xvi.

[5]Herman Melville, *The Confidence Man* (New York: New American Library, Signet Classics, 1964), p. 119.

[6]Hannah Arendt, *Eichmann in Jerusalem* (New York: Viking Press, 1963).

[7]Henry Adams, *The Education of Henry Adams* (New York: Houghton Mifflin Co., 1918), p. 312.

[8]Counting only the names of Jeremiah's contemporaries who appear in the narrative, about sixty persons are named. It is not possible to be precise in the number as in two or three instances the names may be variants referring to the same person. Sixty names, plus or minus two or three, seems to me to be an extraordinary number in so brief a narrative.

Chapter 14: I Bought the Field at Anathoth

[1]John Fowles, *The Aristos* (Boston: Little, Brown and Co., 1964), p. 50.

[2]Even in the realm of philosophical discourse—not, it would seem, a highly practical field—we have made our distinctively American contributions in thinking about how to make things happen, in understanding how things get done. The pragmatism of William James and the instrumentalism of John Dewey steered a wide berth from anything resembling an ivory tower and have pursued the down-to-earth concerns of the practical person. "It is no exaggeration to say that in American intellectual life irrelevant thinking has always been considered the cardinal sin." John E. Smith, *The Spirit of American Philosophy* (New York: Oxford University Press, 1963), p. vii.

[3]"I was talking to David Riesman a few weeks ago, and he was saying that apocalyptic solutions and apocalyptic analyses and diagnoses don't interest him, really, because it's the little things, day by day, picking up the garbage in this village, that makes life *work*, and the values will finally take their shape from these thousands of little efforts, of little decencies, little organizations that give the *ground* for social continuity." *Robert Penn Warren Talking*, Interviews 1950-1978, edited by Floyd C. Watkins and John T. Hiers (New York: Random House, 1980), p. 192.

[4]Coventry Patmore, *The Rod, the Root and the Flower* (Freeport, N.Y.: Books for Libraries Press, 1968), p. 52.

[5]G. K. Chesterton, *Heretics* (London: Bodley Head, 1905), p. 114.

[6]William Stringfellow, *An Ethic for Christians and Other Aliens in a Strange Land* (Waco, Tex.: Word Books, 1976), p. 138.

[7]George Eliot, *The Mill on the Floss* (New York: The Century Co., 1911), p. 409.

[8]Philip Reiff, *The Triumph of the Therapeutic* (New York: Harper & Row, 1966), p. 37.

Chapter 15: Concerning the Nations

[1]Arend Th. Van Leeuwen, *Christianity in World History*, trans. H. H. Hoskins (London: Edinburgh House Press, 1964), p. 100.

[2]D. T. Niles, *Upon the Earth* (New York: McGraw Hill Co., 1962), p. 250.

[3]Ernest Becker, *The Denial of Death* (New York: The Free Press, 1973), p. 74.

[4]Quoted by Niles, *Upon the Earth,* p. 259.

[5]A possible, though not at all probable, exception is recorded in chapter 13 in the story of the linen waistcloth. Jeremiah is instructed to "go to the Euphrates" to bury it, which he did. If, in fact, this is the River Euphrates, it was a 700-mile round trip. The word in Hebrew is *perath* and, though used often for the Euphrates River, more likely refers to Parah (modern Ain Farah) about four miles from Anathoth where there is an abundant supply of water. Since Parah and Euphrates were very similar in sound, the former could have stood symbolically for the latter. Indeed "to Parah" and "to the Euphrates" would be spelled identically in Hebrew. See Thompson, *The Book of Jeremiah,* p. 364, and Bright, *Jeremiah,* p. 96.

[6]Marianne Moore, *Predilections* (London: Faber & Faber, 1956), p. 12.

[7]Bright, *Jeremiah,* p. 307.

[8]Kenneth Cragg, *The Call of the Minaret* (London: Oxford University Press, 1952), p. 183.

[9]André and Pierre-Emmanuel Lacocque, *The Jonah Complex,* p. 30.

Chapter 16: In the Land of Egypt They Shall Fall

[1]William Foxwell Albright, *From the Stone Age to Christianity* (Garden City, N.Y.: Doubleday, Anchor Books, 1957), p. 402.

[2]Friedrich von Hügel, *Essays & Addresses on the Philosophy of Religion,* 2d series (London: J. M. Dent and Sons, Ltd., 1926), p. 54.

[3]Karl Barth, *Epistle to the Romans* (London: Oxford University Press, 1960), p. 327.

[4]Flannery O'Connor, *Mystery and Manners* (New York: Farrar, Straus and Giroux, 1961), p. 94.

[5]The tidy conclusion that the book of Jeremiah fails to give is supplied extra-biblically (as it usually is!) by the first-century *Lives of the Prophets.* A most satisfying ending is provided by combining a hero's honor among the Egyptians and a martyr's death at the hands of the Jews: "He was of Anathoth, and he died in Taphenes in Egypt, stoned to death by the Jews. He is buried in the place where Pharaoh's palace stood; for the Egyptians held him in honor, because of the benefit which they received through him. For at his prayer, the serpents which the Egyptians called *epoth* departed from them; and even at the present day the faithful servants of God pray on that spot, and taking of the dust of the place they heal the bites of serpents." Charles Cutler Torrey, *The Lives of the Prophets,* Greek Text and Translation (Philadelphia: Society of Biblical Literature and Exegesis, 1946), p. 35.